Kirtley Library
Columbia College
Columbia, Missouri 65216

for Executive Action

Douglas C. Basil

American Management Association, Inc.

© American Management Association, Inc., 1971.
All rights reserved. Printed in the United States of America.

This book may not be reproduced in whole or in part
without the express permission of the Association.

International standard book number: 0-8144-5247-7
Library of Congress catalog card number: 79-138565

FIRST PRINTING

Preface

TODAY'S MANAGERS rely more on the human resources available to them than managers at any time in the history of complex industrial organizations. The education and sophistication of even the most menial employees in an affluent society require the manager to have an ever more highly developed set of leadership skills. These skills can be developed only through an understanding of human behavior in organizations.

The purpose of this book is to provide a précis of the current knowledge about human behavior, not in the sense of the psychologist studying abnormalities, but rather in a pragmatic and useful manner that will help the manager to understand both himself and those with whom he must deal in his business career. An organization is designed not only to accomplish work, but also to provide human satisfactions and an outlet for emotional and psychological drives. The manager who fails to understand that the business organization is as much a social entity as it is a means for achieving economic goals is doomed to failure.

The author develops the thesis that neither the leader nor the followers controls the destiny of the organization. Rather, it is the interaction of the leader with each of his followers, with groups of followers, and with the economic and social situation which will determine the effectiveness of the leadership supplied to the organization. Authority can be a hollow shell because, although it is conferred on the manager by organizational fiat, it may not be acceptable to his subordinates. Power, not authority, makes an organization work toward its goals.

What motivates men to build bridges, eradicate disease, and produce toys, automobiles, and all the commodities required by an advanced industrial society? Economists tell us that it is private gain or profit. But what does profit mean to a man who already has millions more than he can spend in twenty lifetimes? What motivated John F. Kennedy to become President, Robert McNamara to become secretary of defense, or Nelson Rockefeller to become governor of New York State? And what motivates the assembly-line employee to be punctual or to meet production standards? Obviously, motivation is a complicated process which is not easily stereotyped or understood. Motivation must be individual in nature and dependent upon particular needs and desires at a specific point in time. To motivate successfully, the manager needs an understanding of the employee's attitudes and background, or of his frame of reference. But this understanding requires the leader to develop his skills of empathy (or seeing things from another's point of view), and to devote his time and energy to listening to his subordinates.

This book emphasizes the behavioral aspects of management to complement the managerial considerations raised in the author's companion volume, *Managerial Skills for Executive Action* (published by AMA in 1970). That book develops the critical factors involved in structuring an organization from the viewpoint of division of tasks, allocation of responsibility, line and staff, and the like. *Leadership Skills for Executive Action* develops the critical factors involved in decentralization, delegation, and the behavioral implications of management controls. Together, these two volumes provide a guide to executive action which considers both the managerial and the leadership skills required for organizational effectiveness.

Special attention is devoted to communication, not only in one-to-one situations but also in conference leadership. We say far more than we realize when we communicate. The slightest gesture, facial expression, or even the way we look at another person results in far more telling and often harmful communication than we ever intended. The manager, as a leader, communicates either as a sender or a receiver perhaps 70 percent of his working day. The quality of his communication can make the difference between a willing acceptance and understanding by subordinates, peers, or superiors, and their reluctance or misunderstanding.

Leadership skills do not come naturally to most managers, and need to be consciously developed. Every manager has experienced failures caused not by his inability to plan or make decisions, but by his lack of understanding of human reactions and interactions. The development of leadership skills need not produce an oversensitivity to human actions and a softness of management decision making. But it will develop an appropriate sensitivity which should greatly reduce management errors.

The accent in this book is on the pragmatic application of leadership skills to the solution of managerial problems. The reader will develop a deeper understanding not only of human beings and human behavior but also a set of skills which should hold him in good stead as a practicing manager.

Douglas C. Basil

Contents

1	Understanding Human Behavior for Leadership	1
2	The Social System and Leadership Skills	22
3	Human Motivations, Incentives, and Leadership Patterns	41
4	Behavioral Patterns in Organization Structure	63
5	Delegation and the Practice of Leadership	75
6	Behavioral Patterns in Management Controls	98
7	Effective Communication for Leadership	112
8	Conference Leadership	134
9	Developing Leadership Skills	156
	Selected Bibliography	185
	Index	189

1

It is not enough for the manager to utilize managerial and technical skills in performing his function. He must also apply leadership skills, since his effectiveness depends directly on the human actions and reactions of his subordinates.

Understanding Human Behavior for Leadership

HISTORICALLY, the emphasis on scientific management, productivity, and efficiency on the production line created a management attitude that treated human and nonhuman resources alike. A man was considered essentially interchangeable with a machine. Like a machine, he could be bought, sold, or scrapped. The social and economic environment was such that the scarcity lay in the supply of jobs, not in the supply of labor.

Management philosophy and practices developed on the premise that labor was a commodity just like any other. Management itself was not treated any differently from labor. There was little or no recognition of individual differences among human beings. Management assumed little or no responsibility for the development of the individual, and motivation was considered to be strictly a function of financial reward. Management made the decisions, and labor carried them out.

It would be expected that, as the social and economic environment changed, management would develop new philosophies and

1

practices. All too often, however, management has not provided this leadership, and in many instances organized labor or government action has been used to force management to change its practices. When management forfeited the initiative in effecting change, the new decision parameters greatly constrained the flexibility of operation of the firm.

Now management is again on the threshold of a new era. The technological and sociological changes which will occur in the decades ahead are almost unimaginable. They threaten not only the survival of management itself but also all institutions of private enterprise. The ever-increasing literacy and higher standards of education of all men, both those in labor and those in management, coupled with an enormous increase in the standard of living, make obsolete many of the premises on which management built its theories and practices. Therefore, management must create new theories based on an understanding not only of the all-important technological changes in production processes and management methods, but also of human resources, which are perhaps even more complicated than their physical counterparts.

Human Aspects of Leadership

To meet these technological and sociological challenges, every manager must develop both appropriate leadership and interpersonal skills and managerial and technical skills. (The terms "leader" and "manager" will be used interchangeably because it is assumed that an effective manager must also be an effective leader.)

Effective management requires leadership. Leadership in a business organization, which can be a nonvoluntary organization, is more difficult than leadership in a voluntary organization, which is one a man can join or leave without financial hardship, such as a church, social club, or recreational group.

Leadership in business is more difficult for two reasons. First, the autocratic nature of the business enterprise results in the appointment of the manager, rather than in his natural selection or election by his followers. Second, the relationship between the leader and his followers in the business enterprise is essentially nonvoluntary, because the leader is required to motivate his followers to a much higher degree than in the voluntary organization.

These two factors do not create ideal conditions for effective leadership. In fact, they throw the major responsibility for the relationship on the leader rather than on the followers. Nevertheless, the contrary opinion underlies the thinking of modern managements.

The manager tends to believe that his subordinates are responsible for relating to him and, in effect, for pleasing him in order to succeed in the organization. This is a false premise. It is the manager who reaps the greatest reward from the effective performance of his subordinates, and therefore from his part of the total organization. It is also the manager who suffers most from the ineffective performance of his subordinates. This line of reasoning points to the need for a change in the manager's attitude toward his subordinates if he is to be an effective leader, and to the importance of leadership skills and an understanding of human behavior, as well as of managerial skills.

Management pays lip service to the need for what is usually termed human relations. Many firms approach this need by sponsoring special courses on supervisory training, often even entitled "Human Relations," as an integral part of a foreman training program. Although management undoubtedly recognizes the importance of the human factor, the accent is all too often placed on manipulation of human beings to make them feel happy while they help the firm achieve its objectives. The term "manipulation" is used here to mean the motivation of a man to accomplish a task by implying that the task is in his best interests, when in fact its greatest benefits apply to the manipulator. Eventually even the least sophisticated employee realizes that he is being manipulated; the result is loss of confidence in management and a decrease in the quality of human relationships in the firm.

For example, a research director in a relatively large organization practiced manipulation as one major means of managing his employees. He was a handsome, smooth-talking man who, although he had a Ph.D., had failed to keep abreast of developments in his field. This was not to his discredit, since his administrative responsibilities did not give him time to devote to research. However, he was in the unenviable position of having to satisfy a management which was basically unsympathetic to research activities while simultaneously meeting the needs of his research staff to engage in projects of interest to them.

Because he did not really understand the problems of management or the complexities of the research projects, he followed management's instructions to the letter, and used his persuasive powers to convince each researcher on his staff that the project was in the researcher's best interest. He did this by implying that a particular line of research would lead to the publication of articles in the professional journals as well as to recognition by management. Actually, however, he neither knew nor believed that any given project would lead to either result. Everyone except the newest researchers soon realized that the research director was using manipulation. His staff began to distrust him, and the research laboratory had the highest turnover rate of any laboratory of its type in the country. In addition, the majority of the researchers lost confidence in management in general.

Effective leadership does not require the manager to be a psychologist. In fact, the case could be made that the psychologist would be a poor manager because of his ignorance of other aspects of the management process. To be effective, however, the manager must understand human behavior. Many successful managers have evolved effective leadership patterns merely through a high degree of sensitivity to human interactions, although in psychological terms they do not know why they deal with their subordinates in certain ways. In contrast, a highly placed manager who has attained his position through family connections, or even through an unusually high degree of technical skill, may be unable to deal effectively with others. However, his subordinates may have evolved patterns of followership to compensate for his lack of effective leadership patterns. If this manager had the ability to establish good interpersonal relationships, he would undoubtedly be able to attain an even higher position in the firm.

A knowledge of human behavior is required if effective leadership is to go hand in hand with effective management. This knowledge need not be technical in nature, but should enable the manager to gain some understanding of human motivations, aggression, and needs, and the role of empathy in dealing with other human beings.

Perception and Leadership

Everyone uses perception every day. In order to perform the many activities of everyday life, most people develop a high degree of competence in confronting a physical world replete with sounds to be interpreted, obstacles to be avoided, and distances to be estimated.

The social world is no less demanding or confusing. It includes unknown or partly known people whose motives must be judged, whose influences must be estimated, and whose interrelationships must be determined. Adequate progress and success in the world depends in large part on the accuracy of social perception. The person who is unable to perceive social interactions has difficulty adjusting satisfactorily to the world.

Because the manager is responsible for motivating and coordinating others toward attainment of objectives, his inadequacies in social perception are often tantamount to failure. He needs not only managerial skills but also the ability to perceive the social behavior of both subordinates and superiors. Every day he faces new social situations, even in his well-established human relationships. He must sense the feelings of his subordinates, become aware of the actions required to satisfy their needs, and determine what difficulties he will experience in utilizing their talents.

Research by psychologists on perception indicates that the success of a leader is a function of his ability to satisfy the needs of his followers.[1] In order to satisfy those needs, the manager must first become aware of his subordinates' feelings and psychological makeup. To do this, and to evoke effective performance from his subordinates, the manager must be able to relate to his subordinates both individually and as a group.

This goal is a hard one to achieve; furthermore, the manager may have difficulty drawing the line between adequate servicing of his subordinates' needs and dangerous meddling in their lives. Men have fought for centuries to gain privacy and freedom of thought. Moreover, each man adjusts to the world and his environment on the basis of his previous experiences, and most people build up psychological

---

[1] Graham B. Bell and Harry E. Hall, Jr., "The Relationship Between Leadership and Empathy," *Journal of Abnormal and Social Psychology* 49 (January 1954), p. 156. See also Treadway C. Parker, "The Psychological Environment and Work Group Behavior," *Personnel Administration* 27 (September–October 1965), pp. 26–31.

defenses to compensate for their inadequacies. The manager must exercise great care to avoid interfering in private lives or disturbing the equilibrium which others have developed for themselves.

The question of how far the manager can go in probing his subordinates must be determined early in his relationship with them. They must believe that his interest does not invade their privacy and that they have no reason to distrust his motives. In addition, the relationship must not go so far that the follower becomes emotionally dependent on the leader.

Although the manager needs to train himself to increase his social perception of others, he must also recognize his limitations in analyzing their actions in the business environment. Even if he were extremely skillful in social perception, he would have neither the appropriate relationship with his subordinates nor the necessary time for in-depth analysis. The danger for the manager lies in inadequate observation, which can result in unsatisfactory analysis and conclusions.

A major asset of the manager trained in social perception is his greater accuracy in predicting the reactions of his subordinates and others to various business decisions and actions. Within the latitude allowed him in the managerial hierarchy, the manager can take actions which result in the satisfaction, or at least partial satisfaction, of his subordinates' needs. When organizational constraints force the manager into taking actions which his subordinates may resent or reject, his social perceptions will put him in a much better position to anticipate their reactions, and thus to placate them and satisfy their needs in some other manner. Although a tendency to manipulate is always present, the use of social perception is far more effective in the long run. People differ widely in their social perception of or sensitivity to the feelings of others, which naturally leads to the question: Is perceptive ability innate or acquired? At one time, psychologists believed that perception was independent of learning, but more recent studies have indicated that perception is a function of experience and therefore can be learned.[2] The trend toward study of human relations, both in industry and in the universities, seems to support this thesis. The increased use of sensitivity or T-group seminars to develop deeper social perception and

[2] Joe Kelly, *Organizational Behavior* (Homewood, Illinois: Richard D. Irwin, 1969), pp. 477–487.

sensitivity is indicative of the increasing belief that perception can be a learned skill.[3] There is definite evidence that it can be acquired through a lifetime of experience or, to a more limited degree, through classroom study.

Despite these findings, even a casual observation of the business world reveals that managers as leaders do not pay sufficient attention to the feelings of others. This attitude may reflect underlying traditional management philosophies. The term "businesslike" connotes in common usage the separation of the logical and rational aspects of issues from the human or illogical. Business prides itself on being practical, divorced from the seemingly irrational needs and actions of human beings.

This belief has resulted in the evolution of a series of business mores in which attention to the personal factor is seen as a managerial weakness. It is difficult to cultivate social perception in such an unnatural environment. Human beings are greatly influenced by other human beings, and human feelings do influence so-called rational business decisions. The wise manager recognizes the impact of such human interactions and sharpens his perceptive abilities to manage these human interactions to his advantage.

The Limits of Authority

It does not take long for a manager to realize that authority can be a hollow thing. Although the formal organization establishes his authority over his subordinates, this arrangement assumes that such authority can be determined by the formal managerial hierarchy. In reality, authority is established only through the relationship between superior and subordinate, and not through the arbitrary action of anyone outside that relationship. There are few jobs where the interaction between the manager and the subordinate can be ordered automatically. Even in the most mechanical type of job, certain discretionary areas are open to the subordinate's interpretation. It is the use of this discretionary action which may very well make the difference between the efficient and the inefficient worker.

To insure effective action by the subordinate, the manager must

[3] Chris Argyris, "T-Groups for Organizational Effectiveness," *Harvard Business Review* 42 (March–April 1964), pp. 60–74.

not depend solely on the hierarchical, authoritative relationship between them; instead, he must motivate the subordinate to do a superior job. To understand what motivates a subordinate, the manager must comprehend his psychological needs by practicing social perception. However, it is equally important for the manager to analyze his own motivations, to perceive himself in his own environment. It is not only success in the sense of material possessions or prestige which motivates the manager; every manager wishes to be creative, in the sense of achieving some goal.

One measure of such creativity in the business firm is the manager's ability to attain his given objectives. A second aspect of creativity lies in the fact that the manager fulfills himself only by fulfilling others. In other words, he accomplishes nothing by himself, because his act of creation occurs only through his management or coordination of the acts of others. Thus, much of his sense of accomplishment comes not only from attaining his objectives in a material sense, but also from fulfilling and satisfying his subordinates in their accomplishments.

The average business situation is replete with conflict, but if conflict marks the relationship between manager and subordinate, both will find it difficult to attain personal satisfaction from work. Adequate social perception and the motivation of subordinates to fulfill their needs and desires will give the manager a bonus for his work: personal satisfaction derived from pleasant interpersonal relationships. The manager is caught between pleasing his superiors and his peers, or pleasing his subordinates. With social perception and an understanding of human behavior, he can go a long way toward satisfying both groups. When he sees social perception in this light, the problem is not whether he should become sensitive to the feelings of his subordinates, but how he can train himself to achieve that sensitivity.

Understanding Human Behavior—The Hierarchy of Needs

Many managers tend to base their philosophies and practices of management on a series of false premises about human behavior. One major mistake they make is what psychologists call projection. The manager projects his own feelings and attitudes into his interpretation of the actions of others. He assumes that all people have his motivations and interests. Nothing could be further from the truth. Everyone has different experiences from everyone else. Even two brothers have different experiences in the family situation, if only because one is older. If the manager is to be successful as a leader, he must learn to eliminate unsound practices such as projection and to understand the basic tenets of human behavior.

Basically, human behavior is devoted to the satisfaction of needs. Life is essentially a cycle from unsatisfied needs to satisfaction or goal achievement, repeated time after time. As one goal is achieved, a new need, usually of a higher order, arises. Where satisfaction is static, motivation is nonexistent, which means the end of the learning process, of improvement, and of innovation. The satisfaction of needs does not always require total attainment. Need satisfaction can be achieved through expectations for the future as well as through shorter-range goals.

The identification of needs is a necessary but difficult task for the manager. Each man establishes a hierarchy of needs which not only changes frequently, but is rarely known even to himself. The writer's experience in eliciting statements of corporate and personal objectives from middle and upper managers in executive development programs supports this statement. It was obvious that each manager had a hierarchy of needs and was highly motivated to satisfy them. Few, however, had explicitly determined what those needs represented in either a business or a personal sense.

If a man has difficulty determining what his own need pattern is, it is certainly far more difficult for the outsider to ascertain that pattern. Yet, the key to understanding human behavior is the recognition and identification of these needs. It is believed that man's hierarchy of needs is determined by his psychological and physical situation at any given time. In ascending order, such needs are:

1. Physiological needs such as food, water, and sex, which enter little into the average work motivational pattern of twentieth-century Western man.
2. Safety needs such as protection from harm and some guarantee against economic deprivation.
3. Social needs such as acceptance, recognition, prestige, and respect.

4. Internal needs such as opportunity for personal growth, and self-fulfillment or personal satisfaction from one's endeavors.

The greatest difficulty in utilizing such a hierarchy of needs is that people have a number of needs simultaneously and are often unaware of which provides the strongest motivation. Furthermore, certain needs such as money are not simple but complex. Money can represent a desire for prestige or for safety, or even for self-fulfillment when economic independence allows a man to express himself completely without worrying about the consequences. The manager must be careful to distinguish the varying motivational needs of his subordinates so that he will be able to offer them the maximum motivational opportunities available within the confines of his job responsibilities.[4]

Human Needs and Management Action

The failure of the manager or the organization to satisfy the needs of an employee may go relatively unnoticed by both the manager and his subordinate. However, the widespread failure of business organizations generally to motivate people through the satisfaction of needs creates a feeling of apathy in employees which leads them to seek satisfaction through sources other than work. The following example emphasizes the importance of motivation in leadership and management.

A scientist who had recently completed his Ph.D. was vitally interested in doing research in his own field. In seeking a permanent position, the scientist was far more interested in his research opportunities than in pay, location, and other factors normally of considerable importance to newly graduated scientists. He joined a firm and usually came to work an hour and a half or two hours earlier than anyone else. He frequently spent his evenings and other free time reading extensively in the literature. Aside from fulfilling his family obligations, he devoted his entire life to his scientific research.

He soon found, however, that his personal research ambitions were of little importance either to his supervisor or to the company.

[4] Frederick Herzberg, "One More Time: How Do You Motivate Employees?" *Harvard Business Review* (January–February, 1968), pp. 53–62.

His experience and training in the field indicated to him that a number of profitable research opportunities were available, but little heed was paid to his interests. Before long he left the firm to seek his ideal in another situation. Four jobs and ten years later, he had failed to find the niche that would satisfy his personal research ambitions. Finally, apathy replaced zeal. Now he apathetically follows orders, no matter how inane he considers the project to be. He no longer goes to work early or reads widely in the literature of his own field. He has turned his attention from research to music, one of his earlier interests in life. Undoubtedly he is a capable, but mediocre, research scientist. But this situation was not all of his making. Management in a number of leading companies failed to understand his needs and to motivate him to greater accomplishment through the satisfaction of those needs.

By seeking employment in another firm, this research scientist took overt action to protest the organization's inability to satisfy his needs. All too often, however, the employee does not articulate his dissatisfaction to precipitate a crisis. Rather, his output gradually slows down and his apathy toward his work increases. Management often fails to recognize this behavior as a symptom of its inability to satisfy the needs of the employee. Instead, it views apathy as characteristic of the working man in general, an attitude which leads to many miscalculations in dealing with employees and lower levels of management. The manager looks outward toward his subordinates rather than inward for explanations of mediocre or poor performance. He is inclined to blame employees for lack of drive, rather than to blame himself for failure to motivate them to performance that will provide the recognition and satisfaction they desire.

Attempts to identify needs are further complicated by the search for simple, logical explanations of behavior. What seems to be a striving for financial reward may in fact be simultaneous needs for status, recognition, and achievement. If the subordinate exhibiting an extreme interest in money is categorized solely as a materialistic being, the result may be that he receives inadequate incentives to motivate him. The manager must not oversimplify the need structure of his subordinates, but rather must realize that each is seeking numerous rewards simultaneously.

Needs themselves are determined by personal, institutional, economic, and social factors. Obviously the need structure of workers in underdeveloped countries is far different from that of workers in the more advanced nations. Furthermore, the need structure even within one culture constantly changes as mores and social customs change.

As each generation enters the industrial sector, its forefathers fail to understand its needs and motivations. Many of today's top managers grew up in the Great Depression of the 1930s, and entered the managerial ranks during the privations of World War II. All too often today this same top management group fails to adjust to the needs of the high school and college graduate of the 1960s and 1970s. The older manager had to strive hard for even a semblance of security; for today's college graduate, the Great Depression and World War II are historical facts, certainly of note, but not of his experience.

The recent graduate has had experiences which are essentially unknown to the older manager. He has grown up in a period of strong and emerging centralized government. He has known the inevitability of the draft without the accompanying patriotism of World War II. He has been raised in an age of nuclear power, which, although not necessarily a part of his consciousness, has nevertheless affected his personality growth.

These differing experiences have resulted in very different need structures for the two groups. Each has a responsibility to attempt to understand the peculiar background of the other and to do what is necessary to satisfy the other's needs. But the onus for understanding must fall on the older managers, because it is they who must motivate the younger group through identifying and satisfying the latter's needs.

A further complication enters here. The business firm develops not only one-to-one relationships, but also relationships between groups and individuals. Some of the employee's needs are determined essentially by the group rather than by himself. Where group needs differ drastically from personal needs, strife and inadequate adjustment by the employee will result.[5]

[5] Warren C. Bennis, "Organizational Revitalization," *California Management Review* 9 (Fall 1966), pp. 51–61.

Thus, the manager must be cognizant of both group needs and individual needs, because satisfaction of the latter may be difficult or impossible without satisfaction of the former. Again, the manager will face the difficult problem of ascertaining group needs when they are not overtly determined, even by the group itself. Furthermore, the manager as a leader must not overemphasize the group to the detriment of any of its members.

Another major obstacle to identification of human needs is the fact that they are psychological, social, and personal in nature. Even if the manager is able to understand and isolate human needs, all too often he approaches their satisfaction through rational, intellectual action. This approach is doomed to failure. The manager must recognize that rational behavior will not necessarily solve emotional problems with or between subordinates.

One illustration of the buildup of an emotional problem occurred in a university when an assistant professor presented his resignation. Unwilling to lose such a promising young faculty member, the dean asked the man why he was leaving. He answered that he was not only to receive a higher rank and a larger salary in his new position, but also that he expected to have greater opportunities to advance his professional stature.

After the interview, the assistant professor told a friend that he dreaded leaving the university. He said that he was highly satisfied with his classes, his colleagues, and almost everything else about the university, and he added that his wife and family were content in the community and apprehensive about moving to a less important institution. His friend, perplexed by these statements, said he did not understand the resignation. At this point the true reason for the assistant professor's action came out. He had written a number of articles and books, and performed various services for the institution. He felt he had done as much as anyone to receive promotion to the rank of associate professor, and that the failure of the dean and the university to reward him for his past services had prompted him to accept a position in another institution.

His colleague then supplied some special information which the assistant professor apparently had not known. He indicated that the dean was under intense pressure from the administration and other schools in the university which made it impossible for him to fight for a promotion for this man at the time. The assistant professor responded to this information by saying that if the dean had explained this situation to him before he resigned, and had asked him to wait another year for a promotion, he would have been content to stay. He also said that even if the dean were to explain the matter to him now, he would be unwilling to remain.

The need which the dean should have identified was that of recognition. The assistant professor really cared very little whether he received a promotion this year or next. What he did require was recognition of his worth. The dean's failure to understand this need lost him an excellent faculty member.

The manager deals with human behavior which has as its base what might be considered irrational behavior—actions which seem to the observer inappropriate to reach the stated or apparent objective of the person concerned. The objectives of the assistant professor were professional development and recognition. To the outside observer, it would be obvious that he could better achieve these objectives in his present position; therefore, his actions could be considered irrational. But such behavior is irrational only when the observer fails to understand human behavior and motivations. The fact that a subordinate is acting irrationally is of little consolation to the manager. He must coordinate the actions of the people under his supervision to attain an objective. That attainment is possible only if it will satisfy the needs of all concerned, rational or irrational.

The Search for Recognition

The evolution of modern society has deprived the individual of the psychological security of feudal times, when society was essentially static. Elaborate caste or social hierarchies assigned to each man his position and task in life. Although today we would decry this lack of mobility and individual freedom, the very orderliness of feudal society created its own psychological rewards. The guild system set forth rigorous requirements for its members which gave a form of social recognition perhaps known today only to medical doctors. Furthermore, the division of labor had not yet reached the point where each person was responsible for only a part of a job; therefore, the worker, and the tradesman in particular, could receive personal satisfaction and recognition from his job.

Sociologically, modern man in the Western world, and in the United States in particular, is immersed in a sea of democratic equality. Great mobility exists between social classifications, and even they are not clearly defined. No longer is birth the key to social patterns and security. Benchmarks for social recognition undergo constant change. During the first few decades of the twentieth century, the accent was on gaining social status or position through money and the things money could buy. This denominator is now no longer strictly applicable. Education is fast replacing money as society's measure of the worth of the individual, but even within education the accent has alternated between the cultural advantages of a liberal arts education and the practical advantages of engineering and scientific training.

Psychologically, the twentieth century has also caused a series of new problems for the individual, who must define his role in this complex new world. In feudal times the worker knew what his task was and received personal satisfaction from its accomplishment. He could see his relationship to the small and rather narrow world of his existence. If he was a shoemaker, he patterned and manufactured the shoe, carrying the process through from measurement of the customer's foot to final fitting of the shoe. For this task he received the recognition which every human being so greatly desires. Furthermore, the strict ordering of society gave this tradesman a sense of security because he knew he would be making shoes for the rest of his life. Little anxiety or tension was directly connected with his work.

The point here is not that feudal society was good and modern society bad; rather, it is that the psychological and sociological problems of people are greatly magnified by modern technology and its effect on society. Certainly no one would deny that the flexibility of social classes, the availability of education to all, and the right of the common man to determine the course of history are all great leaps forward for mankind. But these achievements have not been without cost. Men have great difficulty adjusting to the gigantic changes which now occur with great rapidity and frequency.

For all his education, man is still man. Even the most sophisticated is bewildered by modern technology and society.

Certainly some companies and many managers have recognized the importance of the individual's search for recognition, but much of this understanding has been intuitive rather than the result of a conscious, planned action by management. For example, all too often the manager's overdependence on financial incentives is effective, not because of the incentives themselves, but because they symbolize a form of recognition. It is true that the accent on human relations in business has increased, but even a casual observation of the average firm will reveal management's neglect of the extremely strong need for recognition. Boy Scout badges, the extensive hierarchy of fraternal organizations such as the Freemasons, and the elaborate trappings of the military all attest to that need.

The industrial organization has many opportunities to grant recognition to its employees, and should consciously exploit the individual's search for recognition. "Exploit" in this sense means to utilize to the fullest. As long as the manager is not guilty of manipulation, this exploitation will lead to benefits for the subordinate, because he will gain more satisfaction from work; for the company, because he will be more productive; and for society, because higher productivity leads to a higher standard of living.

However, the search for recognition may also hold dangers for the organization. Recognition can become so important to a man that he will fight any change in organizational practices because of its potential effect on his recognition as a person of worth. Man is often overprotective of his prerogatives, not necessarily because of selfishness or callousness, but because of his fear that these prerogatives will no longer serve as recognition devices. Furthermore, recognition by the institution, being essentially impersonal, has limitations. In the long run, it is still the manager, in his interpersonal relationships with his subordinates, who has the greatest impact on the satisfaction of their search for recognition. Praising a competent employee in the presence of his peers, writing a personal letter of commendation, or offering a few words of encouragement will contribute to the satisfaction of that need. Of course, such recognition must not be given lightly. It must be earned and must be approved by the group, although such approval is usually tacit rather than overt.

Opportunity for Self-determination

The search for recognition is one of the strongest of the hierarchy of needs of most people. But as mankind evolves higher patterns of culture and civilization, and technological advances give him greater material rewards, man moves toward the very end of his continuum of needs, namely, self-fulfillment. Recognition is essentially a group process; the acknowledgment of one's work by others gives satisfaction. Self-fulfillment, on the other hand, is a personal matter.

The power of the group and of society in general to determine and condition behavior is indeed strong. Even in such a mundane matter as the style of clothes, few will break the rules of society. Men wear lapels on their coats and narrow or wide ties, as the times dictate; the length of women's skirts goes up and down with the whims of Paris and New York designers. The approval or disapproval of the group and society acts either to bestow or to withhold recognition of the individual.

Every human being, however, has the capacity to go beyond the censure or praise of the group, or even of society. He can demand the right of self-determination or self-fulfillment. History is replete with such men who, through the need for self-fulfillment, took unpopular actions for the good of all. They were condemned by the society of their day, and recognition and approval were withdrawn. Yet most of them were vindicated by history.

Modern industry, through its managerial structure, implicitly offers people opportunities to receive recognition through position in a hierarchy—but those opportunities are often just as automatically denied in the same hierarchy. Organizational structures are established for the objective of minimizing errors while at the same time allocating tasks. Because the allocation of tasks to various parts of the organization has as its base the specialization of labor, the opportunity for the individual to achieve self-fulfillment is even more difficult. He is identified only with the part, not with the whole. It is often difficult for him to fulfill himself if he cannot relate his work to the end product of the organization. Of course there are certain assignments, many of them of a staff nature, which give the manager ample opportunity for self-fulfillment. In addition, if he understands and accepts the rationale of the organization and its constraints, he can concentrate his energies toward that ultimate goal.

The trend to decentralization implicitly, although not necessarily explicitly, recognizes the human need for self-determination. Because of the ever-increasing layers of the hierarchy in larger firms, central management finds it difficult if not impossible to make decisions relating to the various parts of the organization. The decision to decentralize authority may be made solely on the pragmatic grounds that the organization has become too large and unwieldy for strict centralization. Or the decision may be based on the premise that actions can be taken more effectively by local or lower-level managers than by centralized management dependent on long lines of communication.

There is a contrary trend toward centralization based on the argument that the computer can analyze data and permit centralized decision making. From a behavioral point of view, such centralization will decrease motivation and lead to apathy or sabotage. In other words, the individual manager is in a better position than centralized management to know the needs of his part of the organization. He will also have more recent and perhaps more detailed information on which to base his decisions.

The concept of decentralization was developed as a technical managerial technique to solve the problem of organizational rigidity and inflexibility caused by size or distance. Its development did not consciously consider human needs or human behavior. Yet it could be argued that psychological reasons are equally or more important in decentralization of authority than are the technical considerations of communication.

Most people feel lost in a large organization. They find it difficult to see how their work contributes to the whole. They are upset by the bureaucratic mechanisms which run the business. As a man rises in the managerial hierarchy, he often becomes more frustrated in his desire for self-fulfillment. The constant battling he must do merely to have a decision accepted by top management, or to have a decision of theirs rescinded because of its inapplicability to the local situation, soon wears down his motivation to achieve self-determination. After a time many managers feel they cannot beat the system, and sink into apathy.

When a firm truly decentralizes authority, the manager has within his grasp the opportunity to satisfy his urge for self-fulfillment. This motivational factor helps make decentralization successful. It is as important as the technical processes of decentralized data collection, which lead to better decisions on the local level.

Behavior Patterns and Leadership in Review

In dealing with the human factor in the management equation, it seems obvious that the manager as a leader must understand human behavior. But we need only look at the divorce courts, the law courts in general, and everyday life to realize that most people have an inadequate grasp of human behavior. Furthermore, such understanding is not merely a matter of knowledge and understanding; wisdom and skillful practice are also required.

Perception based on an understanding of behavior is part of the process of acquiring skill in human relations. Fortunately, the whole world is our laboratory for practicing perception. Countless times every day we have opportunities to improve our perceptive skills at work, at home, and in social situations. When a conflict arises, or an unsatisfactory human relationship develops, we should analyze the reasons. This process requires a degree of objectivity about our own behavior which is difficult to acquire.

There are times when even well-developed skill in human relations and leadership will not necessarily resolve conflicts caused by role identification, such as those involving policeman and criminal, teacher and student, or sales manager and budget director. Such conflicts can be minimized by understanding human behavior, but they cannot be eliminated.

For example, a role conflict might develop between a vice-president of engineering and the controller in a firm. The vice-president might wish to incur costs for a program which was not forecast in the budget. The controller would determine the expenditure and revenue situation, and might in effect veto the expenditure through his influence and position. Highly perceptive managers who are well qualified to understand the management process would undoubtedly recognize the fact that this conflict is not one of human relations but of role identification. Nevertheless, the conflict would remain unresolved and would require recourse to higher echelons of management for solution.

The manager who can recognize role conflict will be able to distinguish between those conflicts he can resolve or avoid through perception and an understanding of human behavior, and those which are inherent in the structure of his organization. He will also be able to minimize the potential interpersonal conflict when its cause is role conflict.

Because the leader must motivate his followers to contribute to the achievement of tasks, he must visualize three separate entities in the organization: the individual, the group, and the individual as affected by the group.

Although the leader is responsible for motivating his subordinates, the task of motivation is complicated by the interrelationships between the individual and the group to which he belongs, as Figure 1-1 shows. The leader develops motivational patterns which recognize the influence of the group on the individual's motivations and needs. The result is that the group influences the leader. For example, the leader of a Boy Scout troop would sense the influence of the group on any one scout before attempting to motivate him through some special assignment or task.

The leader must consider the group mores both as they affect his relationship to the group, and as they affect the individual and his

Figure 1-1
Leader-Follower Interrelationships

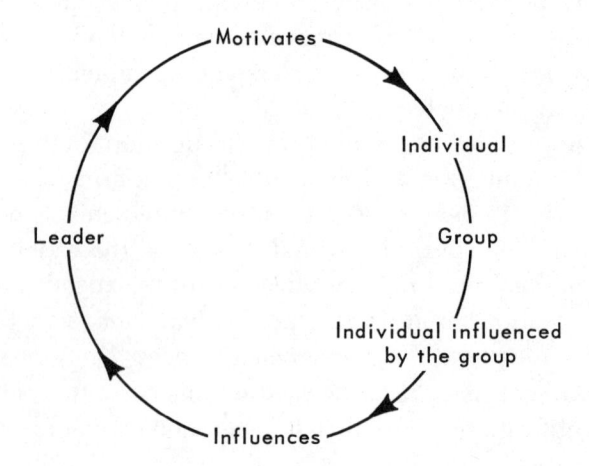

behavior. At this point, each man's search for recognition comes to the fore. He may seek his recognition solely from his group membership and reject any form of recognition from the leader. The soldier, and especially the draftee, may place a much higher premium on acceptance by his group than on the formal trappings of rank or privilege available from his officer.

It is important to understand the special forms of recognition which exist in society and especially in the business firm. Status, influence, prestige, authority, and power all play important parts in the social system of the firm, which is the subject of the next chapter.

2

A business enterprise is simultaneously a separate entity and part of a larger social system. The firm has its own peculiar environmental conditions, mores, or customs, but these internal factors are themselves conditioned by the external factors of culture and society. The manager in his role as leader cannot order relationships and conditions as if no considerations existed except those internal to the firm. Rather, he must be cognizant of the larger frame of reference which will condition those internal relationships.

The Social System and Leadership Skills

Two separate views of organization—the formal management, or internal, view, and the sociological, or external, view—should be integrated to increase the effectiveness of the business firm. The formal basis for organization is a division of tasks into subparts, each of which is assigned to an individual or group. To attain conformity and some assurance that the task will be completed, a management hierarchy is superimposed on those responsible for carrying through the assignments, and serves the organization by establishing channels of communication and channels of responsibility.

In designing an organizational structure, management is oriented toward task accomplishment, which in turn is related to the technical processes involved and the allocation of the necessary resources. To achieve its goals, management determines the optimum size of the working group in terms of efficiency, productivity, stability, or quality for each task.

The sociologist would approach the structuring of an organization in a totally different manner. His objective might be the same as management's, namely, task attainment. He would be interested in observing the cultural, behavioral, and environmental factors affecting the members of the group, but his major interest would be studying the group in terms of its members' interactions, the structure of relationships, and the types of stress which would be likely to arise.[1] Management's task orientation is not wrong, but it must be expanded to incorporate an understanding of these psycho-sociological aspects of organization.

Psycho-sociological Factors Affecting Organizations

Psychologists and sociologists have studied individual and group relationships as one of the focal points of their disciplines. Numerous experiments, most of them fragmented to permit the isolation of variables, have been conducted on human behavior in organizations. Management can learn a great deal about this subject from behavioral scientists, who have established that larger groups are less stable, have more difficulties in communication, tend to inhibit individual participation, and create greater stress.[2] In some instances, the case can be made that a larger group will be more successful than a smaller one because of the greater number of skills available.

Sociologists have noted some special characteristics inherent in small groups: (1) more time is available for each person to test his ideas directly through overt participation; (2) a less clearly defined problem can be attacked; (3) greater pressure exists to participate,

---

[1] Elias H. Porter, "The Parable of the Spindle," *Harvard Business Review* 40 (May–June 1962), pp. 58–66.

[2] John K. Hemphill, *Group Dimensions: A Manual for Their Measurement*, Ohio State Bureau of Business Research Monograph No. 87 (Columbus: Ohio State University Press, 1956), p. 27; Eugene Kaczka and Roy V. Kirk, "Managerial Climate, Work Groups, and Organizational Performance," *Administrative Science Quarterly* 12 (September 1967), pp. 253–272.

and nonparticipation is more evident; (4) feelings of intimacy permit freer expression; (5) motivation is greater, although there are fewer potential resources; and (6) every member of the group can exert a greater influence.[3]

A special case can be made for the formation of groups even when each person is capable of performing his task alone. The presence of other people doing similar types of work can be stimulating, with a resulting increase in productivity of all workers. This advantage is lost as the size of the group increases, since each member feels less important and thus less essential to the group, less responsible for its performance, and less motivated. When the work is repetitious, and therefore requires little two-way communication, the group size can be larger because the need for interaction is minor.

The determinants of size in the problem-solving group differ considerably from those of other groups. The manager faces the dilemma of how to maximize the number of resources to be applied to the solution of the problem and to minimize the reduction in interaction potential that comes with increasing size. The optimal size of the problem-solving group depends upon the number of unique skills each member possesses and the degree to which the communication network is complicated by size and the interaction potential. When the elapsed time to solution is the primary consideration, even problems that could be solved individually should be given to groups.[4]

Studies also indicate that the more heterogeneous the group membership, the better the solution to the problem. But such heterogeneity exacts a price, because the difficulty of coordinating problems increases astronomically. As groups become larger and more heterogeneous, the cost in time and difficulty of attaining consensus increases drastically.[5] The solution to this problem is to have homogeneity in the personality characteristics that are conducive to

---

[3] Herbert A. Thelen, *The Dynamics of Groups at Work* (Chicago: University of Chicago Press, 1954), p. 63. See also Bernard P. Indik, "The Relationship Between Organization Size and Supervision Ratio," *Administrative Science Quarterly* 9 (December 1964), pp. 301–312.

[4] William M. Evan, "Toward a Theory of Inter-Organizational Relations," *Management Science* 11 (August 1968), pp. 217–230.

[5] John W. Thibaut and Harold H. Kelly, *The Social Psychology of Groups* (New York: John Wiley & Sons, Inc., 1959), p. 239. See also Ralph M. Goldman, "A Theory of Conflict Processes and Organizational Offices," *The Journal of Conflict Resolution* 10 (September 1966), pp. 328–343.

interaction effectiveness, concurrently with obtaining heterogeneous skills.[6]

Studies to determine the quality of decisions and the degree of member satisfaction show that a six-man group performs most consistently at an acceptable level of quality. As the group grows larger, each member of it needs to be separately convinced by argument when the adequacy of a solution is not self-evident. The result is an excessive expenditure of time for decisions and a tendency to compromise. Group satisfaction decreases as the size of the group increases, because members of large groups think they are too hierarchical, centralized, and disorganized, and that their members are too aggressive, impulsive, competitive, and inconsiderate. The larger group creates more stress in individual members and more difficulties in communication and inhibits individual performance. When the group is too small, however, discussion is prohibited for fear of alienating other members.[7]

Integration of the Managerial and Sociological Views

Management and the sociologist share one objective in viewing the organization, namely, the effectiveness of the group in task accomplishment.[8] (The terms "efficiency" and "effectiveness" do not have standard, accepted definitions. Barnard defines "efficiency" in terms of the degree of satisfaction of group members, and "effectiveness" in terms of task attainment.) The sociologist, however, views organization in terms of groups and their characteristics, while the manager thinks of organization more as an entity with major technical and managerial constraints. He believes the size and constitution of the group should be dictated by the technological processes involved, and he tends to organize people by function.

These organizational constraints are not as limiting as they may seem at first. It is possible to form subgroups even when technical conditions require larger groupings. The manager who knows how

[6] "Birds of a Feather Produce Together," *Business Week* (March 23, 1957), pp. 115–116.

[7] Harold J. Leavitt, "Unhuman Organizations," *Harvard Business Review* 40 (July–August 1962), pp. 90–98.

[8] Chester I. Barnard, *Functions of the Executive* (Cambridge, Massachusetts: Harvard University Press, 1958), p. 19.

to form a group that will attain both task and member effectiveness in a manner similar to that advocated by the sociologist will find it possible to structure his organization to his advantage. Although many managers unconsciously take many of these group effectiveness factors into consideration in planning organizational structure, a more conscious recognition of their usefulness would result in even greater effectiveness. Most managers have sufficient institutional authority to decide how to form groups within their own parts of the organization.

The group is one of the most powerful forces in society. The manager's control over the organizational structure gives him the opportunity to channel this power into a constructive force toward the attainment of organizational objectives. To do this, however, he needs to develop a much deeper understanding of groups and group relationships.

Authority and Power in the Industrial Environment

The traditional attitude toward authority has undergone considerable change in management theory. Management has been inclined to look at authority solely in terms of the organizational structure and subsequent formal organizational relationships, and to believe that authority and responsibility must be commensurate. There can be little argument with this proposition as it stands; obviously it is useless to assign a task to a manager and then not allocate him the necessary resources to carry through his assignment. The only question is whether authority is assignable. If management can grant authority, the implication would be that its conferral would permit its recipient to have control over, and be able to determine, the behavior of others.

Barnard recognized the inconsistencies inherent in such a definition of the term "authority." He differentiated institutionalized authority, or that granted by hierarchical positions in the organization, from what might be termed authority of leadership, or that granted the individual by personal prestige, ability, and similar factors.[9] At some time in every manager's career, a situation arises which drives home this differentiation.

[9] Barnard, op. cit., p. 165.

One such situation occurred early in the writer's experience. In preparation for an invasion in World War II, regimental commanders culled from their regiments soldiers they considered unsatisfactory for a number of different reasons. These troops were to be reassembled into reserve battalions. The author, with a number of others, was assigned the task of reorganizing these men into a new unit. Although he had each man's army record available, he decided to conduct personal interviews in order to give each soldier as much freedom of choice of assignment as possible. This procedure worked quite well, with one notable exception. His name, oddly enough, was Churchill. When asked what he wanted to do, he replied in a negative and sarcastic way that he wanted to do nothing. The interview continued in this general tone until the soldier was arrested and sent to the guardhouse.

Although the writer, as an officer, had the institutionalized authority to relieve the soldier of his liberty, he apparently did not have the power to secure compliance with his orders.

Sociologists differentiate between authority and power in order to explain the basis of society itself. The relationships among individuals, between individuals and groups, and among groups are not haphazard. They are structured and organized by society, and accomplished by power. Without power there could be neither organization nor order. Power is the latent ability to employ force which underlies to some degree all relationships within society. Society establishes authority through its organizational structure as the institutionalized right to employ power, but this authority is not necessarily synonymous with power itself.[10]

These sociological concepts apply to the business firm as well as to other institutions. The managerial hierarchy is the institutionalized authority structure of the business firm. That authority *may* also be power, because the individual manager has the ability to apply sanctions even to the point of severing the relationship between his subordinate and the organization.

Another dimension must be added to the sociologist's concept of power and authority. The business enterprise, as the primary means by which society accomplishes its marshaling of resources, must necessarily be task oriented. This orientation requires the firm's

[10] Jack H. Nagel, "Some Questions About the Concept of Power," *Behavioral Science* 13 (March 1968), pp. 129–137.

members to observe behavior patterns which will lead to task accomplishment. The use of force through power and institutionalized authority will not necessarily result in the development of those behavior patterns.

In the illustration about the soldier named Churchill, the institutionalized authority was rejected, and even the use of force did not change his behavior patterns to assist in the attainment of the organizational objectives. The translation of authority into power involves not only the organizational hierarchy but also the individual and his relationship to the organization. The introduction of this dimension into the power structure may be implicit in the sociologist's definition of the concept. He may explain this phenomenon merely by stating that the locus of power in the industrial organization rests in the managerial hierarchy. In actuality, it could rest instead with informal groups of workers, with the union, or with a number of people in the organization not formally designated as power holders by the managerial hierarchy.

The reality of organizational life is that the granting of institutionalized authority through the managerial hierarchy does not necessarily carry with it the assurance that such authority will be translated into power patterns which will elicit the behavior patterns needed for attainment of the objective. A major gap may exist between the granting of the institutionalized authority and its actual acceptance by those responsible for carrying through the action. Authority in this sense becomes something granted by the subordinate to the superior; that is, the latter is permitted to influence the behavior patterns of the former.[11]

The important lesson for the manager to learn from behavioral science is that the mere granting of institutionalized authority will not necessarily result either in a change of behavior patterns in those who facilitate task attainment, or in automatic task attainment itself. Certainly, the granting of institutionalized authority is a necessary prerequisite in a formal managerial hierarchy. However, when such authority breaks tradition, results in the change of per-

[11] This phenomenon was discussed almost 50 years ago by Mary Parker Follett, "The Psychology of Control," in *Dynamic Administration*, edited by H. C. Metcalf and L. Urwick (London: Management Publications, Ltd., 1941). See also Robert V. Presthus, "Authority in Organizations," *Public Administration Review* 20 (Spring 1960), pp. 86–92.

sonnel, or threatens the existence of people in the organization, it may be refuted by members of the firm. When these conditions arise, a number of other factors—prestige, status, influence, and the like—will be involved. The manager can ascertain the presence of these factors, but only rarely can he grant them.

When the granting of institutionalized authority is of a routine nature, it will generally be accepted as a matter of course. Because changing officers in the army is commonplace, obeying the commands of the new officer on the parade square will be automatic. But in a battle situation, where the replacement of officers may still be commonplace, the authority of the officer in battle will be questioned until he has proved his leadership abilities. In other words, acceptance of authority is not automatic in this case; rather, it is dependent upon other factors.

A parallel situation can occur in the business firm. Barnard stated that a subordinate, in addition to understanding the communication and being able to carry out the assigned task, must believe that the task is neither inconsistent with the purpose of the organization nor incompatible with his personal interests. He develops a "zone of indifference" as a guide to whether he accepts or rejects the task assignment. Within this zone of indifference, he rarely questions the order from his superior.[12]

The sanctions available to the industrial organization in forcing compliance on its members are limited to severance from the firm. This fact restrains the firm's latent use of power. It is much easier for a man to reject authority in the business world in Western countries than in the political settings of countries such as Russia. Furthermore, the impact of the sanction of severance is drastically limited in a full-employment society, where a man can find another position with relative ease. Even when an employee fears the sanctions of an organization, compliance through fear is at best a negative motivation. He will do as little as possible to the point where the sanctions come into play.

Thus, the manager cannot rely on institutionalized authority as his major means of task assignment and accomplishment. Rather, he must motivate his subordinates through his understanding and satisfaction of their needs. This approach does not obviate institution-

[12] Barnard, op. cit., pp. 165–168.

alized authority; instead, it indicates to the manager that he must generate the leadership abilities necessary to match this granting of authority in order to obtain the power to fulfill his task.

The Social System

The social system applies equally to business firms and to society at large. Factors such as influence, status, and prestige are as much a part of the social system of business as they are of society in general. Although there are definite differences in the meanings of these terms, they all relate to the social system, to power, and to authority.

Influence is the ability to persuade others to follow a course of action. It is not necessarily granted through the institutional hierarchy, although position in the latter may contribute to it. Influence is won by its holder, because it is granted by the one who is influenced to the one who influences. It is not necessarily recognized formally in the institutional hierarchy. It may lead to power, but its hold is less tenuous than that of authority, which is the institutionalized right to employ power.

The business enterprise, as one of society's institutions, can confer status on a man. Because work is man's major activity, society naturally recognizes status conferred through work relationships. Within business, considerable emphasis is placed on status.[13] In fact, the trend is toward a more formalized and rigid corporate caste system.

Esteem or prestige, which will be used interchangeably, differ from status because they are not necessarily granted by the institutional hierarchy.[14] Prestige may accrue to a person because of his character traits, knowledge, wisdom, or even physical strength.

The differences in these terms may be illustrated by the political structure of the United States. The President is granted institutional authority by his election and the Constitution. This authority can

[13] Vance Packard, *The Status Seekers* (New York: David McKay Company, 1959).
[14] The sociologist differentiates between esteem and prestige because esteem may accrue solely to the individual and prestige to the position he holds. See Charles Perrow, "Organizational Prestige: Some Functions and Dysfunctions," *American Journal of Sociology* 66 (November 1960), pp. 335–348.

The Social System and Leadership Skills

lead to power and action. However, the checks and balances of the American political system limit the translation of the President's authority into power, since only Congress can introduce legislation. If the President wishes to initiate action, his status as Chief Executive is insufficient. He must rely on his prestige (gained perhaps from his past actions and the fact that he won the popular vote) and on his influence (gained perhaps by the political plums he can apportion to members of Congress), or on a special mandate from the people through public opinion.

Past Presidents have no institutionalized authority and no formal status because they have no position in the government. But they may have considerable prestige and influence, even to the point of negating some of the proposed actions of the incumbent President.

Figure 2-1 presents a model of a social system which sets forth two routes to power and action. The relationships are oversimplified in order to obtain workable definitions for this chapter.

Route I is granted by the institutional hierarchy: authority begets status which provides a base for power (possibly either prestige or influence or both) which leads to action. Route II is separate from the organizational hierarchy and is won by the individual: prestige begets influence which provides a base for power and leads to action. It is also possible to proceed to power without authority in Route I, or to prestige in Route II. The social system of the firm is composed of all these elements. Each has a separate connotation for the man-

Figure 2-1
Social System Relationships

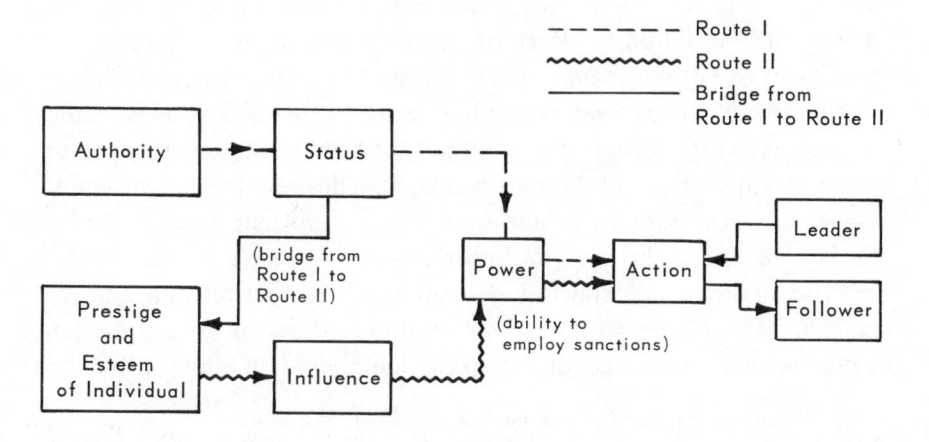

ager, who must be able to recognize all the routes to power and action.

Status in the Business Enterprise No

Status is a natural outgrowth of the managerial hierarchy. Management can provide status symbols by conferring a title, allocating an office, or even assigning responsibility. But just as society or its members may reject authority, so the conferral of a title or position may not result in status for its recipient. It is common in industry to see peer disapproval of management action in promoting or appointing a man to a higher place in the hierarchy. If management continues to take action which is considered inappropriate by the majority of the employees, it will lose its ability to confer status on people.

The keen student of management and of society in general may well ask whether the concept of status is useful to society. The answer is definitely yes. The essence of society is structure, and institutionalized authority and power lie at the root of this structure. But society requires some clearly visible markings through status to insure its orderly functioning, just as visible badges are required to indicate ranks in the military hierarchy. Status requires some form of ranks, which in turn requires a series of value judgments, many of which are of a collective nature. Status is an inevitable concomitant of any stable organization.

Most people covet status to some degree. The manager can and does use this fact as a motivational device.[15] Status is not something to be conferred lightly. If status is truly valued as a scarce commodity in the organization, its achievement can be a more effective motivator than financial reward. For many people, it is not the financial reward itself which is important but the status attached to it. In the hierarchy of human wants, the desire for recognition is one of the most impelling. Status confers recognition, since it testifies to the world that the organization recognizes a man's worth.

The existence of status in an organization permits an orderly pattern of communications. The granting of status to a function where such status is acceptable to the members will elicit automatic

[15] "Executive Trappings," *Time* 65 (January 24, 1955), p. 8.

acceptance of the formal channels of communication. It will also permit persons or institutions unfamiliar with the organization to deal effectively with it by imputing status to members of the organizational hierarchy.[16]

Although both prestige and influence play an important part in the functioning of an organization, status provides a more direct, more visible, and less vague reference. Status hierarchies become organized systems of expectations accepted by all members of the organization. They function to reinforce the natural tendency to venerate major values. These values are made realistic when they are accepted as the traditions of the organization by its leaders, who become arbiters of conduct and behavior for all its members. The resulting dictates of the organization, which are in accord with the accepted status hierarchy, become the standards for determining policy, evaluating individual performances, defining loyalty, and rationalizing injustice.[17]

Although useful and necessary in organization, status is not without its dangers. Status rigidifies the organization to the point where changes are difficult to effect even when they are necessary for the firm's survival. The dictates of human nature, with its tendency to consider change as a threat, plus the difficulty of structuring any organization on unquestionable, unchanging principles or standards of value, result in the status-authority system, which limits the adaptability of an organization. History has proved time and time again that a society's inability to adapt to new environmental conditions is a prelude to decline and disaster. Of all the institutions of society, the business enterprise can perhaps least afford a static system. The dynamics of the business environment demand constant change, but change with stability. Status can be a means to an end for the business enterprise, but it must not become an end in itself. Chester Barnard recognized the pathological aspects of status systems as follows:

1. Tends in time to distorted evaluation of individuals.
2. Restricts unduly the "circulation of the elite."

[16] Chester I. Barnard, "The Functions of Status Systems," in *Reader in Bureaucracy*, edited by R. K. Merton and others (Glencoe, Illinois: The Free Press, 1952), pp. 248–249.

[17] P. A. Munch, *Sociology of Tristan-da-Cunha: Results of the Norwegian Expedition to Tristan-da-Cunha, 1937–38* 13 (Oslo, Norway: I. Hos Jacob Dybwad, 1945).

3. Exaggerates administration to the detriment of leadership and morale.
4. Distorts the system of distributive justice.
5. Exalts the symbolic function beyond the level of attainment.[18]

Management must indeed be careful in its utilization of status and status symbols. They will exist regardless of management's desire to eliminate them. Rather than discouraging the establishment of status, management must use it as a means to task attainment. But when status becomes a block to the adaptation needs of the firm, management must create a new status hierarchy which will assist in effecting change.

The acceptance of status results in a modification of behavior patterns by the employee to accept the authority of the structured nature of the organization. The status symbols are reinforced by the use, or threat of the use, of sanctions plus the assumed legitimacy of the hierarchy. This structuring by the assignment of definite authorities and responsibilities limits the number of stimuli through the status hierarchy, making the predictability and constancy of the response and action of the employee more certain. The status hierarchy demands a constancy of behavior which curtails spontaneity, limits alternatives, and generally defines interpersonal relationships.

Attributes of Leadership and the Social System

Differences in the effectiveness of authority patterns and status symbols can be explained by the differences in backgrounds and the previous conditioning of each person to authority. The employee with a poorer socioeconomic background may have received some form of negative conditioning to authority which makes him reject the organizational environment. An application of sociological concepts to organization classified people into three groups: (1) upwardly mobile people, who identify with the organization; (2) indifferent people, who accept the demands of the organization but isolate their real interests; and (3) ambivalent people, who need the security of the organization but have difficulty playing the role.[19]

[18] Barnard, "The Functions of Status Systems," p. 249.
[19] Bernard Berelson and Gary A. Steiner, *Human Behavior* (New York: Harcourt, Brace & World, 1967), pp. 70–89.

The differentiation between status and prestige or esteem is an important one for the manager. He has the power to confer status symbols on a subordinate, but esteem accrues only to the man who earns it through performance. Homans distinguished between esteem and status as follows:

> ... esteem is not to be had unless a man provides for the members of his group the social values they really enjoy and find hard to come by. Status, on the other hand, makes a man have greater tenure without merit.[20]

Esteem, like status, is a relative measure. It is therefore possible for a man to have high esteem in one group but little or none in another group. Esteem and leadership go hand in hand, although they are not synonymous. The relationship of esteem to leadership has been characterized as follows:

1. A esteems B when he asks B to do something A cannot do. This establishes B as the leader.
2. A asks B to do what both can do equally well. This sets forth A and B as peers.
3. A asks B to do what both can do, but A can do things B cannot. This establishes A as the leader with the power to command B.[21]

In this situation, esteem alone can develop a leadership situation without the necessity of a formal hierarchy.

Both status and esteem are directly related to the predictability of human behavior, and therefore to patterns of conformity. The esteemed man has the greatest potential to introduce change into the group, but he also stands to lose its esteem if the group considers the deviation too great.

To incorporate the concept of esteem into the organizational framework, it is necessary to distinguish between esteem and popularity. In Western culture, particularly in the United States, the emphasis on popularity during the preadolescent and adolescent years puts a much higher premium on popularity for success than is

---

[20] G. C. Homans, *Social Behavior: Its Elementary Forms* (New York: Harcourt, Brace & World, 1961), p. 149.
[21] Ibid., p. 151.

actually the case. Popularity and so-called personality play an important part in company politics and in the reality of success in an organization, but to a lesser degree than many people believe.

The impact of personalities on promotions and job assignments is an all-too-frequent occurrence in industry. Even the formal appraisal system of most firms includes an evaluation of personality characteristics through criteria such as loyalty to the firm and ability to get along with others. This accent on personality factors has led to a high degree of conformity and to the unwillingness of people to disturb the status quo.

Although many observers of the business scene have decried this blatant adherence to the cult of personality, two major considerations lessen the impact of this phenomenon on the effectiveness of the firm. The first factor is that Gresham's Law rarely works in the business organization. Poor employees do not drive out the good ones, but are eliminated when they fail to perform effectively. Such failure is a high cost both to the individual and to the firm. But there is no guarantee that the man who is promoted in spite of his personality defects will be any more successful in a more responsible position.

The second factor which lessens the effect of promotion through personality is the inescapable fact that any managerial position requires the exercise of leadership. Although leadership does not depend solely upon personality, a negative personality will make the exercise of leadership difficult. A pleasant personality and popularity are insufficient prerequisites for a position of leadership.

Very early in the average manager's career he must distinguish among status, esteem, and popularity. His first tendency is to confuse status with the power to exercise leadership and command. He finds that status will assist him in performing his function, but that it is limited to routine actions and may accrue only to the position rather than to him. Another potential mistake is to disregard the factor of status, and instead to confuse esteem and popularity. In taking actions to increase his popularity with his subordinates, the manager may very well lose their esteem. He must consider status, popularity, and esteem merely as means to permit him to exercise influence on the behavior of his subordinates for the purposes of task attainment. The manager must then determine by what means he may best exercise that influence.

At this point the research findings of the behavioral sciences can help to determine the interrelationships of popularity, esteem, and influence. One survey of research findings established that leaders are people who tend to rate higher than average in popularity. The traits found to correlate most closely with leadership were originality, popularity, socialibility, judgment, aggressiveness, desire to accept other people, humor, cooperativeness, liveliness, and athletic ability.[22]

Studies of individuals, although they revealed a positive relationship between prestige or esteem and the extent to which the man was successful in influencing others, found no significant relationship between popularity and influence.[23]

Sociology's lack of a rigorous definition of popularity has made it difficult for the manager to ascertain the worth of these studies. The major question is whether popularity includes both objective and subjective or personal factors. Whyte went to the heart of the matter in his concept of operational leadership:

> The fact that individual Y was elected president of his club tells us something of his popularity with the members. However, it does not tell us that he is an operational leader. He may commonly initiate actions for the other members—but he also may not. All of us can recall cases of elected officers who are merely pleasant figure heads, while other men initiated action within the organization. Now, popularity is worth some study, but we must begin by recognizing that it is definitely not the same phenomenon as operational leadership. The operational leader is likely to be popular, but many popular people are not operational leaders.[24]

[22] R. M. Stogdill, "Personal Factors Associated with Leadership: A Survey of the Literature," *Journal of Psychology* 25 (January 1948), pp. 35–71. See also Warner W. Burke, "Leadership Behavior as a Function of the Leader, the Follower, and the Situation," *Journal of Personality* 33 (March 1965), pp. 60–81.

[23] R. Lippitt Polansky and S. Redl, "An Investigation of Behavioral Contagion in Groups," *Human Relations* 3 (October 1950), pp. 319–348; S. E. Fiedler, "A Note on Leadership Theory: The Effect of Social Barriers Between Leaders and Followers," *Sociometry* 20 (June 1957), pp. 87–94; Zelda F. Gamson, "Organizational Responses to Members," *The Sociological Quarterly* 9 (Spring 1968), pp. 139–149.

[24] W. S. Whyte, "Small Groups in Large Organizations," *Social Psychology at the Crossroads*, edited by J. H. Rohrer and M. Sherif (New York: Harper and Brothers, 1951), p. 298.

A good rule for the newly appointed manager would be to seek esteem or prestige through the exercise of effective leadership rather than through the nebulous route of courting popularity. Leadership depends not on individual traits but on the interrelationship of personality and social situational factors. The ability to provide rare and valued rewards for followers permits both the exercise of leadership and the earning of esteem. These abilities cannot consider only what people want, which may be constantly shifting, but rather the desire of followers to lose their smaller selves in order to find a larger identity in the service of the organization.[25]

Understanding the effect of status and prestige on the functioning of the organization is of considerable importance to the manager. The possession of both status and prestige will normally assist the manager in his interrelationships. He will also be cognizant of the possession of status and prestige by others and of the potential of these factors as motivational devices. Because status in particular is an anxiety-relieving device for its possessor through the implied security it gives, the manager must gauge what effect his actions might have on the status hierarchy in the firm.

Status is often not a consciously planned state of affairs by management, although it may very well be a byproduct of some management action. The following example of management's disregard of existing status symbols will emphasize their importance.

In a small firm, the status of the girls in the office was determined by the relative positions of their desks. The desk closest to the front counter was accorded the highest status because visitors naturally tended to make inquiries of the girl at that desk. When the desks were rearranged to facilitate the flow of work, no desk occupied a more prominent position than any other in regard to the counter. Shortly after the office was rearranged, the girl who had occupied the status desk submitted her resignation, explaining that she had been offered a better job elsewhere. The executives were perplexed by her action because they knew she had turned down several other offers in the past and was one of the highest paid office girls in the town.

One of the executives spoke to the girl at greater length. She

[25] Arnold M. Rose, "The Ecological Influence: A Leadership Type," *Sociological and Social Research* 52 (January 1968), pp. 185–192.

finally said that she was tired of being pushed around and that the other girls didn't accord her the necessary respect. Later, after conversations with the other girls, the executive realized that the previous layout of the office had given status to the girl who quit and the layout change made it necessary for her to leave.

The Social System and Management Action

The manager very quickly learns the meaning of the managerial hierarchy and its implications for his own action. The organization makes certain demands on him for reports, plans, appraisals, and the like. He learns to carry out his management tasks within this formally designed environment.

The manager should also acknowledge the existence of a social system in the firm. Certainly he is still free to effect changes which may run contrary to that system, but he must recognize the consequences of his action and plan his changes so that they will not be refuted by the social system. To operate successfully in this system, the manager must first understand and deal effectively with human beings and then must understand social concepts such as authority, power, influence, prestige, and status. Each of these can complicate or simplify the manager's job.

The manager must understand that status and prestige give their holders the opportunity to exercise influence, which is often the basis of the informal organization and of informal information networks. Influence can be exercised for the good of the company or for the good of the individual, although normally it results in suboptimization, or working toward the goals of a subpart of the organization rather than toward those of the organization as a whole. The man with influence may believe that he is doing what is necessary for the organization, but his limited point of view, experience, and formal position in the organization may lead him to take actions which are not purely in the best interests of the firm.

Influence is a fact of life in political and other organizations. In industry it is often called company politics. The manager may find it repugnant to be involved in company politics, but he should understand these patterns of influence if he is to be successful.

Once he has learned to navigate the seas of human behavior and social systems, the manager is able to steer his course of leadership by the further navigational aids of incentives and motivation. He may be accorded status, esteem, and influence, but he will continue to possess them only through judicious use of incentives to motivate his team. Human motivations and incentives will be discussed in the next chapter.

3

Because each man has a hierarchy of needs which motivate him in all aspects of his life, the manager must be vitally interested in understanding his own and his subordinates' motivational patterns. Motivation itself, however, is a complex phenomenon which cannot be explained solely on the basis of man's need structure.

Human Motivations, Incentives, and Leadership Patterns

M<small>EN TEND TO STEREOTYPE</small> others in order to simplify the external world. Unfortunately, they are inclined to use physical rather than social perception to determine types. Physical perception is a poor guide to the understanding of behavior, but many people judge their fellow men on the way they smoke a cigarette, or whether their eyes are close set. Stereotypes are usually based on false premises relating to past experience retained in the subconscious. A man imputes behavior or motives to another man solely because he resembles someone else with such behavior patterns or motives. In his analysis of the motivational needs of his subordinates, the manager must be careful not to stereotype them, but rather to recognize their complexity.

Motivational Patterns

Viewing human behavior in terms of satisfaction of a hierarchy of needs is an oversimplification which may lead the manager into inappropriate action. A need is a lack of something, which is a negative consideration. The dynamic process of striving cannot be explained solely as the urge to compensate for the absence of something. Motivation involves maintenance of drive or persistence of behavior patterns, not merely identification of a need. Motivation is a function of a complex pattern of stimuli and cognition, determined by both personality and past experiences, and the external environment. Motivation is a phenomenon common to man and animal alike. Organisms tend to maintain an equilibrium of the inner environment in which their tissues live. Whenever this equilibrium, which is called homeostasis, is upset, the organism is motivated to return to equilibrium. If external factors challenge man's inner security, he will be motivated to take action either to increase his internal security or to eliminate the external threats. The identification of a need also upsets a person's equilibrium, motivating him to action to satisfy that need and return to equilibrium.

The terms "motive" and "motivation" do not indicate a simple identification of one stimulus or act, but rather a way to describe a complex pattern of behavior. A man is usually motivated by a number of stimuli at any one time. If only one need is identified, his actions may appear to be irrational. It is this multiplicity of motivations which makes unrealistic the stereotyping of the individual and his motivation or the development of a list of motivational devices.

Two major motivational patterns are found in any social organization, including the business enterprise. The first is submission to the customs and mores of the group and the organization, the ability to conform, or to do what is expected in order to avoid controversy and crticism. Many traditional patterns of leadership in business are based on this type of social motivation. The organization sets forth rules or procedures which members must follow. Failure to adhere to those rules results in disapproval and possibly even a threat to the person's job security.

The second pattern of social motivation is the converse of submission, namely, the active seeking of social approval. This concept is closely related to the need or search for recognition. It is a stronger and obviously more positive motivational device than submission, since the man will do more if he anticipates approval than he will to avoid disapproval.

Motivation and the Individual

Every man must adapt to his particular environment. In business, the usual situation is for the employee to be thrown into an existing environment, which has both technical and human aspects. In most instances, he adjusts quickly to the technical requirements of his job. His adaptation to the human or social environment takes more time and special skills in social perception. He finds that he must not only perceive the frame of reference of the people with whom he works, but must also gauge the unwritten mores and customs of the group or groups to which he belongs or wishes to join. As he adapts himself to his environment, the environment also adapts itself to him. He does have some effect, no matter how miniscule, on others and on the groups in which he has membership. Over time, he reaches a state of equilibrium or adjustment with his environment. He has eliminated or minimized the threat situations and feels secure in his relationships with others in the organization.

The manager is necessarily action oriented. He is interested in eliciting behavior patterns from subordinates which will lead to accomplishment of tasks. If he considers motivation at all—and in many instances he does not consider it or his relationships with others—his inclination is to decide how to motivate the employee to perform one particular task. However, that task often has too little substance to motivate the employee to accomplishment. Even if it results in an immediate financial reward through an incentive wage system, the subordinate does not relate the increased compensation for this particular job to his motivation for its performance. Rather, he thinks in terms of the *total* additional compensation he will reap and its advantages to him. Thus, the manager must relate motivation not to a given task but to the totality of the employee and the organization.[1]

It is a mistake to think that any problem exists in isolation. As

[1] Ernest Dichter, *The Strategy of Desire* (New York: Doubleday and Company, Inc., 1960).

Figure 3-1 shows, the individual problem is affected by a number of considerations, which are depicted as a series of concentric circles. Each circle is superimposed on the previous one, because each factor is affected and conditioned by the others. The largest circle represents the overall characteristics of man; the next, the adaptive characteristics resulting from culture and society; the third, the relationship between the individual and society in general; the fourth, the personal and emotional impact of this particular problem on the individual; and the fifth and final, the problem itself.

Although the manager is urged to understand each subordinate

Figure 3-1
Motivation and the Individual

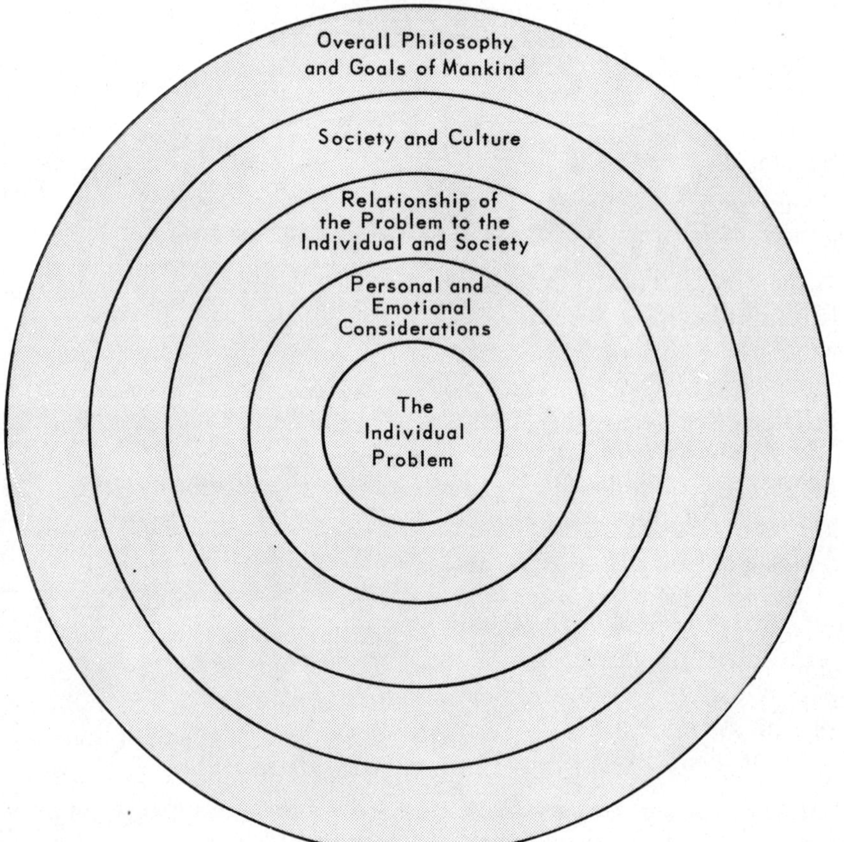

- Overall Philosophy and Goals of Mankind
- Society and Culture
- Relationship of the Problem to the Individual and Society
- Personal and Emotional Considerations
- The Individual Problem

Figure 3-2
Interaction of the Employee and His Environment

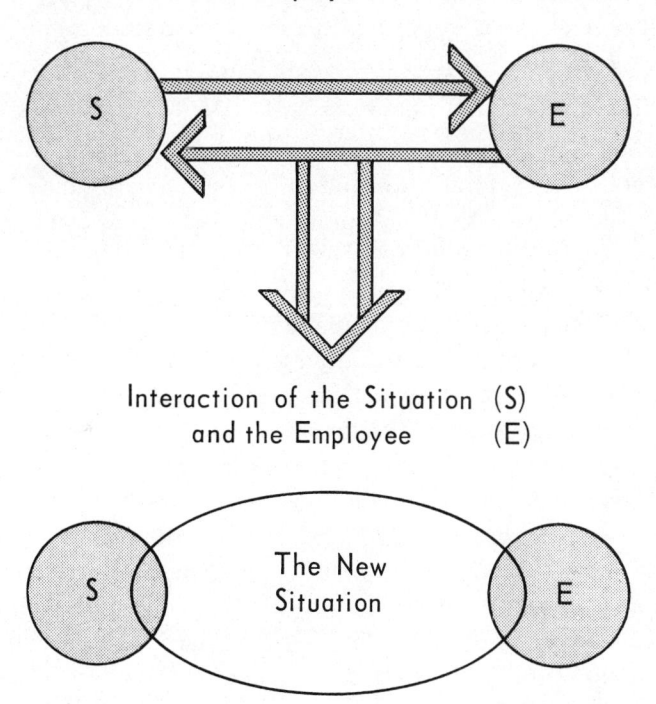

Interaction of the Situation (S) and the Employee (E)

The New Situation

as the key to motivating him, such advice is greatly oversimplified. It is not the employee alone but his interaction with his environment which determines his reaction to any particular incentive. The manager would make a major miscalculation if he disregarded the situation's effect on the employee and devoted his entire effort to understanding the person out of that context.

The interaction of the individual and the environment is depicted in Figure 3-2, where the situation acting upon him at a given time is represented by the circle S, and the employee by the circle E.

To understand the effect of different factors of motivation, it is necessary to recognize that the situation neither acts upon the employee nor he upon the situation. Rather, the interaction of S and E creates a new situation, shown in the figure as a shaded ellipse. This adaptation of the man to his environment and the environment to him is a constantly recurring phenomenon. As the work situation changes or new people are added to the group, this environment or company culture also changes.

The Hawthorne Experiments

Management has been unwilling to recognize the impact of motivation on the conduct of employees and hence on the productivity of the enterprise. Although the most significant findings on this subject became known more than 40 years ago and sounded the death knell of the totally mechanistic approach of scientific management, many thousands of practicing managers have failed to pay heed to these findings. In its attempt to eliminate variables and predict results, management has attempted to depersonalize the organization. Scientific management, with its accent on efficiency, believes that man is motivated only by material considerations and therefore that his actions can be ordered without regard to his personal attitudes and behavior.

The shortcomings of these beliefs were first brought to light in what later became known as the Hawthorne Experiments.[2] They were conducted between 1924 and 1927 at the Hawthorne Works of the Western Electric Company in Chicago. The management was interested in increasing the productivity of its workers. As one approach to this goal, industrial engineers studied the effect of illumination on productivity. Two groups of coil winders were chosen, with one serving as a control group. The illumination of that control group was held constant during the experiment, while that of the other group was increased. As predicted, productivity increased in the latter group, but strangely enough the output in the control group also increased. To test this phenomenon further, the intensity of the illumination was decreased for the test group. The result was another increase in productivity. It became obvious that some factor other than illumination was affecting the productivity of the groups.

The management of the company asked Elton Mayo, a renowned industrial psychologist from Harvard University, to continue this research on changing working conditions and their effect on productivity. Professor Mayo and his associates selected for observation six girls employed in assembling telephone relays. They were physically separated from the rest of the shop and were subjected to a number of changes in working conditions over a five-year period.

---

[2] F. J. Roethlisberger and W. J. Dickson, *Management and the Worker* (Cambridge, Massachusetts: Harvard University Press, 1947). For a more recent critique, see Alex Carey, "The Hawthorne Studies: A Radical Criticism," *American Sociological Review* 32 (June 1967), pp. 403–416.

An observer from the university sat with them to note their reactions. As each new incentive was introduced, production increased. However, when the incentives were removed, output not only failed to decrease to previous levels, but continued to improve. The experimental results of the changes in working conditions and their effect over the five-year period are summarized below.

Changes in Working Conditions	Results
Day work to piece work	Increased output
Five-minute rest periods morning and afternoon	Increased output
Rest period increased to ten minutes	Greatly increased output
Six 5-minute rest periods	Output fell; workers explained that their work rhythm was interrupted
Return to two rest periods, the first with a free hot meal	Increased output
Girls permitted to go home at 4:30 instead of 5:00 P.M.	Increased output
All improvements in working conditions rescinded. Girls returned to 48-hour week, with no rest periods, no piece work, and no free meals	Output increased to highest point recorded during entire period

The Hawthorne Experiments, although inconclusive in providing a blueprint for management action, proved that worker motivation and attitude is a major factor in productivity.[3] The girls who were selected for the experiments felt that the company was interested in them as people rather than merely as cogs in the industrial machine. In response, they produced at a higher rate, essentially to show their appreciation for the special attention. A second factor which motivated them was their sense of belonging to an elite group.

Resistance to Change

Resistance to change is a phenomenon found not only in business but in all areas of life. Kemal Atatürk, in his drive to modernize

[3] Roethlisberger and Dickson, op. cit., pp. 14ff.

Turkey, had to use police action to end purdah and the wearing of veils by Moslem women. The full weight of Mahatma Gandhi's influence was necessary to permit the mixing of the untouchables with other castes in India. In the United States, the power of the federal government has been used to force racial integration. Like these leaders, the manager can no more avoid dealing with resistance to change than he can solve business problems by burying his head in the sand.

If change is an inherent part of life, why do all people, including managers and workers, resist it? Can resistance to change be regarded as abnormal or pathological? One point of view holds that it is more of a symptom than a disease:

> When resistance *does* appear, it should not be thought of as something to be *overcome*. Instead, it can best be thought of as a useful red flag—a signal that something is going wrong.[4]

This statement reinforces the fact that man constantly battles to be in equilibrium with his environment. At one time, his battle was a fight for survival, a need to provide food and shelter for his family. Man still fights for equilibrium, but today it takes the form of making a social adjustment to the people who comprise his work group. That adjustment has both psychological and technical overtones.

In the technical area, each man has some skill to give the organization, which in turn assists him in his social adjustment to the firm. The psychological adjustment is more complex, because it must include the technical aspect as well as the multiplicity of human interactions found in any group situation.

Superimposed on these technical and psychological adjustments is the managerial hierarchy. Since the manager is rarely the natural leader and even more rarely the social leader of the group, he is often considered somewhat of an outsider. When this alien, although accepted, force of the management hierarchy institutes major changes in organizational structure, in work assignments, or in work methods, the group automatically reveals its built-in resistance to change.

[4] Paul R. Lawrence, "How to Deal with Resistance to Change," *Harvard Business Review* 69 (January–February 1969), p. 172.

This resistance is modified by the zone of indifference, or the conditioning of individual employees in the group to accept the orders of the manager. But a subordinate's zone of indifference or area of acceptance is usually limited to routine management actions. He accepts certain actions either because they are routine or because the change will have few personal consequences for him. In contrast, major management decisions rarely fall within the employee's zone of indifference, because they are nonroutine and will have a considerable personal effect on him. They may, in fact, be of vital importance to the employee.

The natural and very human reaction of every man is to consider how each action will affect him personally. The more secure he is emotionally, technically, or even financially, the less subjective and the more objective he can be in evaluating changes initiated by any group in the organization. But rare indeed is the man who does not consider any action subjectively, at least to some degree.

Changes in the cultural environment of the organization are essentially evolutionary in nature rather than revolutionary or radical. When they do occur, they are usually initiated almost subconsciously, internally within the group. The members tacitly agree not to take action which would drastically upset the status quo of the group relationships. Rest assured that there is change, and that over an extended period of time there are drastic changes.

> People do not resist change and they do not resent criticism. They resist *being* changed and they resist *being* criticized, they resist *being* pushed into change and they resent *being* hammered with criticism. But they do not resist change as such. In fact, they accept it. . . . What managers have overlooked, then, is that people really do like change and do not mind criticism if they make these changes and these criticisms themselves.[5]

Most managers, and most other people, rarely have difficulty with unilateral actions and decisions; they experience their greatest difficulties in solving multilateral problems. The introduction of new methods and new organizational structures seems at first glance to be a problem solely within management's prerogative. More

[5] Leo B. Moore, "Too Much Management, Too Little Change," *Harvard Business Review* 34 (January–February 1956), p. 44.

than fifty years ago, Frederick W. Taylor advocated the separation of the task of the worker from that of management.[6] But somehow in this process of evolving a scientific approach to management problems, little or no attention was given to the reactions of subordinates. A logical, well-developed management plan to reduce organizational frictions, institute new labor-saving devices, and replace antiquated methods with modern processes is often actively resisted by employees. When the manager meets such resistance, he is usually perplexed by what he considers a reactionary response to new methods. Usually his solution to this problem is to counter the resistance with additional logical explanations of the advantages of the new methods. He meets with little success because resistance to change is a psychological phenomenon, not a technical dysfunction requiring technical explanations.

To deal effectively with resistance, the manager must recognize the reasons for it. The major issue is usually fear of the unknown and anxiety about how the change will personally affect the individual. If the manager can help the subordinate overcome this feeling of insecurity, he can go a long way toward gaining acceptance of change.

A second reason for resistance to change is that it does not conform to the individual's or the group's view of what is fair or right. In other words, it is alien to the group's mores or customs. The manager must use his perceptive skills to determine whether his contemplated action will be acceptable to the group's mores. Then he must determine what motivation he can use to persuade the group to accept his action. If he finds that his action will probably be rejected, he may have to adopt a leadership role which is highly participative in nature. If the group has sufficient skills and technical abilities, he might find it better to present the problem for group action. Doing this will involve considerable risk; if he must veto the group's decision, he may destroy future teamwork and jeopardize his future leadership potential.

In some situations, even highly developed perceptive skills and persuasive powers are insufficient to overcome resistance to change. The group may be adamant in its belief that the manager's action is not in its best interests or even in those of the organization. The

[6] Frederick W. Taylor, *Principles of Scientific Management* (New York: Harper, 1911).

manager must then decide whether the consequences of disregarding this resistance outweigh the consequences of failing to introduce the change. His decision may be doomed to failure if the resistance is strong enough to defeat the action, but this event would be the exception rather than the rule. Most issues in business are not of a catastrophic nature, and time will heal minor wounds.

Frustration and Resistance to Change

Both frustration and resistance to change are all too often the inevitable byproducts of industrial leadership practices. Frustration occurs when the manager fails to recognize the needs of the employee and to allow him some form of self-development. But frustration in itself is not bad. Without it, there could be no learning. Frustration spurs men to increase their knowledge and develop new abilities. Only when frustration is absolute, resulting in impossible situations, is it bad for the individual and the organization.

The manager is usually in a position to ease or increase the frustrations of his subordinates.

To develop his subordinates, the manager must constantly challenge their existing abilities. Such a challenge is a form of frustration, because it makes the subordinate develop new skills to find solutions to problems for which his present experience and skills are inadequate. The manager usually has the power to determine the work assignments of his subordinates. The manager's task, then, is to determine the level of frustration the employee can endure to permit his development. This determination, plus a judicious use of those assignments, will enable the manager both to simplify his own job and to develop his subordinates.

The Manager and Motivation

In the past few decades, management has shown considerable interest in worker attitudes because it seems logical that a man's attitude toward his job would affect his performance and productivity. If such a relationship could be established, a knowledge of worker attitudes would enable management to predict and measure its effectiveness in motivating workers. Unfortunately, the state of the art as represented by current research does not permit such prediction.

The bulk of the research has taken the form of correlational studies involving high or low morale, high or low productivity, and high or low turnover rates. Although the statement could be made that some relationship exists between job attitudes and output or productivity, the conclusions of these research studies have been far from consistent.[7]

The reason for this lack of consistency is that man may receive his satisfactions from group membership and not necessarily from task accomplishment. The group may not even think of task accomplishment as a source of satisfaction because it has been set unilaterally by management and is therefore considered artificial. There may even be a serious conflict between the goals of the individual and those of the organization.[8] The measurement of the worker's satisfaction or happiness, which can be called his morale, may be related either to task accomplishment or to satisfaction with his group relationships, or even to personal factors related to neither of those. Because any of these variables may be the cause of high morale, there is insufficient evidence to support the use of worker attitude surveys to measure the effectiveness of management action.

There are two major dimensions to work relationships: (1) task accomplishment and individual satisfaction from such accomplishments; and (2) satisfaction with group relationships. Chester Barnard termed a high satisfaction with task accomplishment "effectiveness"; and satisfaction with group relations "efficiency."[9] He developed the thesis that the ultimate goal would be effectiveness and efficiency, and that the route to effectiveness lay through efficiency. This would mean that the employee who was more highly satisfied in his group relationships would also be more likely to be productive.

But here again we must look at the individual and his particular

[7] Rensis Likert, *The Human Organization: Its Management and Value* (New York: McGraw-Hill Book Company, 1967).

[8] Chris Argyris, *Integrating the Individual and the Organization* (New York: John Wiley & Sons, Inc., 1964).

[9] Chester I. Barnard, *The Functions of the Executive* (Cambridge, Massachusetts: Harvard University Press, 1958).

is common in business today, and many articles are written which attest to the traits required for leadership.

Behavioral scientists have attacked the traitist theory on the grounds that the possession of specific traits will not guarantee effective leadership. A high level of intelligence may be a deterrent to the exercise of leadership because the group norms might lead to rejection of the highly intelligent person. If the leader is too different from his followers, biases are built up on both sides which may be difficult if not impossible to eliminate. Moreover, the traitist theory makes no clear-cut distinction between innate and acquired traits; both intelligence and aggressiveness are listed as desirable. However, aggressiveness certainly can be acquired, but intelligence is generally considered to be innate.

Furthermore, the traitist theory holds implicitly that the leader, because he possesses certain traits, will automatically be able to exercise leadership. This belief assumes an essentially static situation, but human relations are dynamic, with constantly changing group relationships and group demands. One situation may demand aggressiveness in the leader, while another situation with the same group may require him to be reticent and unassuming.

For example, Dag Hammarskjöld was a decisive, aggressive and highly successful secretary general of the United Nations. On his death, however, the membership of the United Nations rejected continuation of an aggressive type of leadership. The dichotomy of interests between the Communist bloc and the Western bloc required a leader who would be essentially indecisive and would not give strong support to either position. U Thant, an unassuming type of leader, provided that type of leadership. Thus, it may not necessarily have been the possession of certain traits which made these men successful, but rather their ability to provide the leadership patterns demanded by the situations.

The third generally accepted leadership theory might be termed situational. This theory is an outgrowth of the behavioral scientists' change in thought about environmental or behavioral theories. In its simplest form, the situational theory holds that the situation calls forth the appropriate leader. This theory accepts the findings of the group dynamics experts, who contend that any number of leaders exist in a group, and that the group will choose a particular type of leader for its particular needs. For example, a group of soldiers in a foxhole under enemy fire will choose quite a different type of leader from the one they would select for social reasons back in the barracks. Rather than claiming that leadership is a passive act, the situational theory holds that the skillful leader can adapt to meet the situational needs of his followers. Yet it does implicitly reject the traitist theory that the possession of certain traits automatically leads to effective leadership.

This brief discussion of leadership theories does not do justice to the three schools of thought. Typical advocates of the theories have elaborated and integrated them with more recent findings. Our purpose is not to examine each one in detail, however, but rather to distill from these theories a working knowledge of leadership theory which can be translated into pragmatic practices. This leads to what might be called a composite theory of leadership.

There are effective leaders who cannot be explained completely by either the great man, the traitist, or the situational theory. A recent example is Winston Churchill, who was prime minister of Great Britain during World War II. Churchill did not gain that position until he was more than fifty years old, although he had shown great leadership abilities throughout his career. He was first lord of the admiralty at a very young age during World War I. In 1926, he became chancellor of the exchequer, the top financial figure in the British government. But not until the fall of France in 1940 was Churchill able to reach the ultimate position of leadership in Great Britain.

The great man theory could explain Churchill's success in rallying the British against the Germans. Many people believed that only his indomitable will and leadership skill enabled Great Britain to hold out against Nazi Germany. Advocates of the traitist theory would identify the traits required for leadership of Great Britain and conclude that Churchill's possession of those traits automatically qualified him for leadership. The situationalists might believe that the time of dire need created the appropriate leadership situation, and that Churchill had not been highly successful before 1940 because a special set of circumstances was required before he could rise to his ultimate position.

Undoubtedly Churchill's success was a combination of all these factors. To deny completely any of the theories would be to fly in the face of facts. In the same way, management would be wrong to consider any one of these theories as paramount. The strongest evidence seems to support the situational theory of leadership, but certain facets of the others cannot be denied.

The composite theory of leadership would require the leader to assess the needs of his followers, the peculiarities of the particular situation, past leadership patterns, and the dictates of the organization. His own traits would not become the paramount issue. Rather, the leader would determine what traits are necessary for the particular leadership pattern required to handle the situation.

Leadership Patterns

The leader or manager in business must be task oriented. The organization holds the manager responsible for task accomplishment, and rewards or penalizes him on that basis. The group or team assigned to the manager may be either homogeneous or heterogeneous. The homogeneity may take the form of the possession of similar skills. The heterogeneity may mean the combination of various ethnic backgrounds and social interests. Because work is the major purpose of the group, the homogeneity of skills may be more important than the heterogeneity of social and ethnic factors. The leader has the advantage of work skills in the homogeneous group, but must adjust his leadership patterns to fit the heterogeneity of the group in terms of sociological factors. His overriding task orientation must be tempered with an awareness of both individual differences and motivational patterns, and of group norms and reactions.

Although the subordinates may not necessarily be oriented toward the task set for them, they are still task oriented in their work relationships. Each man seeks self-satisfaction both from his membership in the group, which represents belonging, and from individual task accomplishment, which to a limited degree is an act of creativity. One of the leader's prime responsibilities is the satisfaction of each man's need for creativity through task accomplishment. Some managers are inclined to disregard this need and to become overly involved in teamwork and group functions to the detriment of overall task attainment.

The group members look toward the manager to lead them to task accomplishment. Although conflict may exist between the task set by the organization and that which the group itself would set, the overriding need of the followers for a sense of accomplishment inclines them to support the leader in his task orientation. Although their other great need—the sense of belonging—is supplied by the group more than by the leader, the acts of a leader in industry have a considerable effect on the relationships among the group members. If the leader decrees a series of task assignments which does not permit the group to function effectively as a group, its members will fail to provide internal satisfaction to one another.

The manager needs to recognize the power of the group membership to overrule task achievement. He then has two major responsibilities: he must satisfy his subordinates' needs for task accomplishment, and he must set the stage to permit them to gain a high degree of satisfaction from group membership itself.

In a business or any other organization with a managerial hierarchy, the dictates of the organization are imposed on the exercise of leadership. These dictates act, for the most part, as constraints on the initiative permitted the manager. The managerial hierarchy may force him into a situation which is unpalatable to the group, thus constraining him from choosing a particular leadership pattern even though he knows that it would elicit the greatest cooperation.

The following illustration shows a continuum of leadership patterns, ranging from laissez faire, or complete freedom of action for the followers, to autocratic, or little or no freedom of action. Although some empirical evidence is available on the efficacy of various leadership patterns, it is far from conclusive.[10]

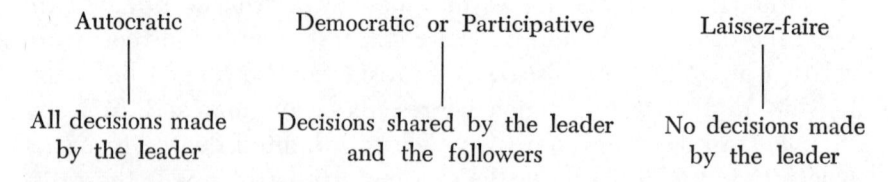

Autocratic	Democratic or Participative	Laissez-faire
All decisions made by the leader	Decisions shared by the leader and the followers	No decisions made by the leader

The correlation of data on groups and group relationships with the laissez-faire pattern of leadership would inductively lead to its

[10] One of the most commonly quoted experiments in efficacy of leadership patterns involved the Boy Scouts, and was reported by Roger Bellows in *Creative Leadership* (New York: Prentice-Hall, 1959). Certainly paucity of information is to

rejection. Even if the group had all the necessary resources to permit effective decision making and action, the very lack of orderliness within the group would defeat its attempts toward task accomplishment. As soon as one member infuses order into the group, he assumes leadership, and the laissez-faire leadership situation no longer applies.

At the other end of the continuum, the exercise of autocratic leadership depends, to a great degree, on power gained through the hierarchy of position. The political dictator is usually autocratic and dependent upon the power of the police state in his exercise of leadership. He makes the decisions and orders, and his followers carry them out. Much of the power of the autocratic leader in a business organization stems from the acceptance of autocratic leadership as one of the mores of organizational life. The management hierarchy of the business organization is autocratic. Although the individual manager is free to determine his own leadership patterns, the responsibility for decision making is placed on the manager, even when staff assistance is used in making that decision.

An excellent case can be made inductively for the autocratic leader. He satisfies the needs of his followers for orderliness and task accomplishment. In business, decisions must often be made quickly and acted upon immediately. The autocratic leader exercises his decision-making power because he has already conditioned his followers to accept them without question. Autocratic leadership reduces the potential tensions within the group because the leader-follower relationship is very strictly defined. The result is a high degree of consistency in behavior, by both leader and followers. This is a main reason why the military has always utilized autocratic leadership coupled with strict discipline.

The major criticism of autocratic leadership is that it does not necessarily call forth the best efforts of all members of the organization. It denies the individual an opportunity for self-fulfillment. His involvement is usually limited because he feels that he has had no part in the decision and only a minor part in the accomplishment of the task.

be decried, but even if more extensive information were available on leadership patterns, it would still prove inconclusive without a depth study of the group, its composition, and the special dictates of the situation. A more recent study confirming this position was made by Fred E. Fiedler, *A Theory of Leadership Effectiveness* (New York: McGraw-Hill Book Company, 1967).

The third type of leadership is termed "democratic," although a better term for business organizations would be "participative," since managers or leaders are appointed in business rather than elected and cannot be removed by fiat of the members of the organization. Although he may reserve the decision-making power, the participative leader motivates his team by eliciting their maximum participation in the decision-making process. Unlike the laissez-faire leader, the participative leader does direct the group and does retain the power of veto over the action of his team. He is more likely to present the problem to his subordinates for decision, rather than to present the decision as a finished product. He actively strives for group harmony and group contribution to the task.

There is no one universally successful pattern of leadership. The composite theory notes that one major variable is the situation, but a slavish adherence to one particular pattern of leadership would fail to recognize this all-important factor. In evolving leadership patterns, the manager must develop the necessary skills to analyze the leadership situation, the needs of his followers, and the dictates of the organization. Usually he will tend to use one pattern of leadership, autocratic or participative, but he will necessarily have to adapt his leadership pattern to suit each situation.

Some special problems may plague the manager in his choice and application of leadership patterns. One problem is consistency. Human beings find a great deal of security in unchanging conditions. If the manager changes his patterns too often and too drastically, his lack of consistency will bewilder his subordinates.

Another special problem occurs with a change of leadership. The leadership pattern used by one manager conditions the receptiveness of the group to the pattern of his successor. For example, the manager may find the participative leadership style unsuccessful for a group conditioned to an autocratic style. The converse is also true. Under such conditions, the new manager may have to assume a leadership style foreign to his own interests until he can recondition the group to accept a different style.

A third special problem which occurs with any choice of leadership style is the type of task or job and the peculiar makeup of the group. In a factory with highly repetitive, machine-paced tasks, the opportunity for participative management is severely limited. The use of that approach to any great extent might even result in worsening the performance and lowering the morale of the workers. On the other hand, a group of research scientists would reject a totally autocratic leadership.

The manager soon recognizes that he must provide leadership for his subordinates. He cannot abdicate his decision-making responsibilities to the group. In choosing a leadership pattern, he must not confuse popularity with leadership. There is a place for participation, but great dangers exist in group decision making. All these factors point to the manager's need to examine all facets of leadership. If there is a formula for effective leadership, it is the ability to gauge the needs of subordinates and of the organization, and to understand the dictates of the situation.

Leadership in Action

The manager is always in a leadership situation. His very title implies leadership, since he must coordinate the work of men toward the attainment of an objective. But a great gap often exists between appointment to a position of leadership and exercise of that leadership. Underlying the relationship between leader and follower or manager and subordinate are human interrelationships. Since each man's behavior is affected by his membership in a group, the leader must relate his own actions both to the group and to the individual.

The group represents society on a small scale. The values of society, as represented by status, influence, and prestige, apply to the group and to its relationship with the leader. The skillful leader can use this social system to assist him in motivating his group toward attainment of organizational objectives. The differentiation of authority from power is also a necessary prerequisite of leadership. The organization may grant authority to the manager, but only through the possession of power can he translate this authority into action. Power, in turn, may involve sanctions granted by the organization, or influence and prestige won by the manager in his past actions with his followers.

The manager must deal with his environment, which is formed on one side by the organizational constraints which the managerial hierarchy places on him, and on the other side by the group mores and customs growing out of the culture of a particular society. Only by recognizing such an environment can the manager motivate the members of his team to put forth their best efforts for him and the organization. But another dimension must be added to the twin constraints of the group or society in general, and the organization. The psychological makeup of every individual differs from that of every other. Each has had different experiences, resulting in attitudes and prejudices which color his view of the world; in addition, the pressures of society and of the group affect each man's behavior. Somehow the manager must navigate this uncharted territory, setting a different course for each member of his team. It is no wonder that leadership skills are difficult to master.

To determine the frame of reference of each team member, the manager must practice social perception, which is based on an understanding of human behavior and in particular on human motivations. But human behavior is complex. The manager who depends too much on his knowledge of the hierarchy of needs, and bases his action on an oversimplified view of human behavior, may cause a disaster. He must integrate his knowledge of human motivation, man's hierarchy of needs, the social system, and leadership theories and patterns in order to analyze and understand the actions of people in the business enterprise.

On the basis of his analysis and understanding of human behavior and of the peculiar situation calling for leadership, the manager can develop his own leadership style *to deal with each particular situation.* Knowledge of the various theories of leadership can contribute to an understanding of leadership patterns and styles, but when these theories are applied to the growth of specific leadership styles, it becomes apparent that the great leaders are those who adopt appropriate leadership styles to deal with their particular situations.

The ability to develop the necessary traits and to exercise the leadership skills required to handle the situation is a prerequisite to success in management. Only through study of human behavior and social systems, and through constant practice in more effective interpersonal relationships in day-to-day contacts can the manager acquire leadership skills and abilities.

In designing an organizational structure, management tends to believe that giving attention to objectives, controls, and other forms of structure will result in an effective organization. But management must recognize that the enterprise is part of society and cannot divorce itself from human needs and motivations. Each man in the organization, whether he be president or janitor, must receive satisfaction from his work and his place in the organization. The structure may be designed for maximum effectiveness, but the individual will insist that it also be designed for maximum human satisfaction.

4

Behavioral Patterns in Organization Structure

Society builds its own social system. The institutions of society are both superimposed on that system and conditioned by it. In the same way, management must recognize the fact that it is not the arbiter of all interaction in the organization, and that its members will mold the organization to achieve their personal satisfaction. Thus, management must design the formal structure to give the greatest latitude for personal satisfaction while simultaneously achieving organizational objectives.

Formal and Informal Structures

The formal organization is usually the creation of top management; the informal, of its members. The formal organization breathes order into the body; the informal, life. Both are necessary for the operation of any enterprise.

Management cannot design the formal organizational structure so that each and every member will find total personal fulfillment of his needs for status, prestige, or work satisfaction. Such a task would be impossible not only because of its magnitude, but also because of the difficulty of satisfying needs through the use of only one structure. The formal organization is at best a compromise, and because man is a social animal who craves the society of others, informal organizations will always exist. They will always be social systems complete with influence, prestige, status, and power.

Utilizing the Informal Organization

People gain satisfaction from interaction with others; therefore, the group, rather than the individual, may determine what satisfies each person. When the formal organizational structure fails to satisfy individual needs, the members of the organization will reshape the structure in such a way as to achieve maximum personal satisfaction. Since this reshaping will occur regardless of managerial action or reaction, management should attempt to utilize or direct the informal structure so that the individual can gain his satisfaction and the enterprise can attain its objectives.

A second factor contributing to the development of informal organizations is the action orientation of management. The manager is given a task to accomplish, and will attempt to do whatever is expedient to fulfill that responsibility. Expedient actions often require other actions or informational contacts outside the formal organizational structure, which results in development of an informal organization. Personal influence, which is not necessarily commensurate with the position granted by the formal structure, may be an offshoot of the informal organization, as the following example illustrates.

The formal organizational structure of one company established channels of authority and responsibility from the vice-president of manufacturing through department supervisors to foremen to lead hands. Superimposed on this structure were the usual staff agencies of production planning and control, purchasing, industrial engineering, and the like. Fairly elaborate procedures and policies were formulated to assist in coordinating the various facets of the manufacturing division.

A special subsection of production control, called subcontracting, was set up to seek work for machining or fabricating in any department where the workload was light. To carry out this assignment, the manager of subcontracting established a direct line of communication with all the foremen and department heads in the manufacturing division. He was a likeable, knowledgeable man in whom everyone had a great deal of confidence. Before long, he was being solicited by foremen for special advice and help. It became known throughout the manufacturing division that whenever any quick action was necessary, the manager of subcontracting could make the arrangements.

This is a concrete example of how an informal organization grew to achieve results not possible through the formal structure. Fortunately, the objective of the informal organization paralleled that of the formal organization, so that no conflict of objectives existed. In many situations a definite conflict of objectives will arise between the informal and formal organizations which must be resolved by management if corporate objectives are to be attained.

The Manager and the Informal Organization

The manager has greater opportunities than the worker for shaping the organization to meet his personal needs for satisfaction. Unlike a worker, whose influence rarely goes beyond his own work group, the manager interacts with a number of other managers and therefore has a much greater potential effect on the entire organization. In most instances, the manager is motivated not only by his personal objectives but also by those of the people assigned to him. He resorts to the informal organization only when the formal structure constrains him too severely in the pursuit of his objectives.

The formal organization may have shortcomings such as lack of information, lack of authority, or slowness of action, any of which makes it difficult if not impossible for the manager to carry out his responsibilities. When this situation arises, he establishes informal contacts and eventually the informal organization to overcome the constraints. Although this informal organization may seem to have the same objectives as the formal one, it is more likely to maximize a different set of objectives.

The danger of the informal organization lies in the fact that its limited frame of reference may cause the manager to take actions which, although he honestly believes them to be in accord with organizational objectives, are in fact contrary to such objectives. And, since the informal organization usually evolves to serve one manager or one section of the organization, its actions may run contrary to the needs of other sections, because little or no attention is given to those needs.

The informal organization, because it is not designed or evolved with the sanction of top management, is the product of unilateral or bilateral action, but rarely involves examination by all parties affected by it. The original design of the formal structure considered the problems of coordination from an overall point of view. The informal organization considers coordination only from the standpoint of the manager who creates the structure.

An additional problem occurs when the informal organization evolves for the purely personal gain of one individual, even if such gain is conducive to the attainment of corporate objectives. Such an informal organization was described by a company president, whose firm specialized in fabricating metal to customers' specifications. The company had a number of standard models but was able to exist in a highly competitive industry by making whatever design changes customers required in the standard models. Because the firm had to compete with both custom manufacturers and standard manufacturers, there was constant pressure on both prices and delivery. The salesman who could promise faster delivery usually obtained the order even if his firm's price was slightly higher than that of a competitor.

The company hired a personable, clever young man as one of its regional salesmen to work out of the plant. There were seven other salesmen, each covering one region. The new salesman soon realized that customers wanted speed of delivery above all other considerations. To achieve that goal, he decided to build his influence within the company to obtain special treatment for his customers. He became extremely friendly with the production control manager, the production superintendent, and most of the foremen in the shop. His experience was sufficiently broad so that he could help and service these company managers.

The new salesman soon had so much influence within the plant that his orders were always given priority over those of the other seven salesmen. His relations with his customers continued to improve. His success was phenomenal, but sales through other salesmen decreased in volume and quality. The president decided that he must either fire the bright young man, who was the best salesman the company had ever had, or watch his organization disintegrate. The salesman was dismissed.

It might be argued that the salesman was more interested in fulfilling his own objectives than in attaining those of the company. Yet the objective of both the organization and the salesman was an increase in sales. The salesman's limited frame of reference was such that he could not see that his actions in setting up an informal organization were detrimental to the health and even survival of the entire company.

The development of an informal organization by operating management usually starts when there is an apparent lack of information or poor communication within the formal structure. Sometimes a manager who wants information for his personal use to gain status in the organization begins acting as a communications center. His major sources of information are secretaries or clerks in sensitive positions working for top management. The unofficial information he gets is often both partial and inaccurate, resulting in discontent and ineffective management action.

In the highly complex, centralized organization, the channels of command are often long and complicated. The field manager who requires information or assistance often creates a special and informal channel through one or two people in the head office. They will be able to give him information informally when the formal organization fails to provide the assistance or information he requires.

The grapevine is usually prevalent in any business enterprise. Sometimes it is encouraged by management as a way to spread information quickly throughout the organization. Yet the use of the grapevine involves the very serious danger that the information will be subverted to the personal use of its recipients. Management should remember the object lesson learned in elementary school, where the teacher whispered a short message to the first student and asked him to repeat it to his neighbor. By the time the message reached the last student, it bore little if any resemblance to the original. The same thing usually happens with the grapevine.

The Worker and the Informal Organization

The worker, unlike the manager, is less likely to be attuned to the needs of the organization, if only because he is not as responsible for attaining the objectives of his part of the organization, which are in turn closely related to corporate objectives. Although the worker seeks personal satisfaction at work just as he does in his outside life, he is usually considered by the formal organization to be like any other resource that is utilized to attain corporate objectives. Management may or may not motivate him in ways that will enable him to experience personal satisfaction. But man does not exist in a vacuum. If the formal organization does not satisfy his needs, he will organize, on an informal basis, groups which will.

Management, in dealing with the informal organization, is usually faced with a *fait accompli*. If the manager determines what this system condones and condemns, he can formulate his strategies to deal with it. With time and patience, he can partially mold the group and partially condition his own actions to accomplish his objectives. The informal organization is constantly in a state of flux; therefore, the manager must be skilled and perceptive enough to uncover and understand this social system before taking action which may run contrary to it. This is not to say that he cannot and will not take actions that are counter to the mores and customs of the social system, but merely that he should be cognizant of the consequences of such actions.

The informal organization, which is developed by both management and workers, is a fact of organizational life. It is not something to be decried or eradicated. Rather, it is a phenomenon of human interaction which management should understand and then utilize to attain organizational objectives.

Roadblocks to Effective Organization

The major roadblocks to effective organization are the vagaries of human behavior, which result in managerial defects. Those responsible for the design of the structure cannot anticipate every organizational problem and, in particular, every clash of personality. Although it is difficult to stereotype typical human problems in a business environment, the following are fairly common.

The Empire Builder. This man thinks that the more people he has under his command, the more important he is. He spends all his time attempting to enlarge his organization, mostly horizontally, and to justify his need for more authority, status, and power. To deal with this man, management should use objective standards of performance which set forth the size of staff required to do a given job. In addition, his superior may be able to modify the Empire Builder's attitude so that he will understand that status is not necessarily enhanced by increasing the size of his organization.

The Eager Beaver. This man tries to do everyone's job except his own. He takes whatever action he thinks will gain him the greatest recognition in the eyes of management, but he often does this at the expense of his colleagues. Objective standards of performance can restrain the Eager Beaver, although the organizational structure itself can restrain him if management enforces definite lines of authority and responsibility. If job assignments are made correctly in the first place, he should have sufficient work to satisfy his personal requirements. The heavy workload, plus the evaluation of his performance against an objective standard, will serve to keep him hard at work.

The Buck Passer. This man is the most difficult to deal with, since any organizational structure must be designed to permit the passing of information to higher authority for decision. To handle the Buck Passer, management must be strong enough to demand that decisions be made at the lower level. When the Buck Passer refers a decision to higher authority, his superior should simply return the information to him, indicating that the latter's decision is in order.

In the case of the Buck Passer, the organization itself is often at fault, if it fails to reward initiative and damns the man who exercises initiative by making decisions. If a man makes a number of decisions on his own and receives only censure, he will be inclined to pass future decision-making situations to superiors for action. To solve this problem, management should demand that subordinate managers make decisions, and should make clear that failure to do so is as grievous a fault as making wrong decisions.

The Power-hungry Administrative Assistant. The position of administrative assistant is usually created to solve organizational problems, not to create them. Yet, when an administrative assistant is given too much responsibility, the result is often that he makes decisions he is not qualified to make, or usurps the power of others. The assistant is in a position to censor his superior's actions and decisions, which have their basis in the information he passes to his boss and the appointments he sets up for his boss.

A typical case of the Power-hungry Administrative Assistant occurred in a large company whose president became so busy that he appointed an administrative assistant both to carry out certain tasks and to act more or less as a personal secretary. The assistant was very capable and soon became the president's trusted adviser. He was not only influential with the president; he was also in a position to determine company action and policy through the appointments he permitted and the information he passed to the president. It soon became known in the company that checking first with the administrative assistant was necessary if the initiator of any action wanted to have it accepted by the president. Thus, the administrative assistant used his position to become as powerful as the president. Although he was clearly not in the direct chain of command, the services he provided for the president permitted him to be, in effect, a decision maker.

Theoretically, the organization handles the problem of the administrative assistant by insisting that the chain of command run through line rather than through staff. However, it is the superior's responsibility to define the relationship between himself and his administrative assistant to insure that the latter does not usurp authority and exercise decision-making power by fiat.

The Staff-Line Man. The staff-line relationship is difficult enough without the Staff-Line Man, who seeks refuge in his staff status but makes line decisions which negate the basic dictum that staff advises, line commands. Theoretically, the organizational structure should have taken care of this problem by defining its staff and line relationships, but this is difficult to do. The problem lies in the fact that knowledge is power, and power permits decision making. The staff man is highly specialized and qualified in a particular specialty and is responsible for advising and assisting the line. His knowledge of the particular subject is usually much greater than that of the line man who is responsible for the decision. As a result, a powerful personality in a staff position can in effect make decisions. The problem is that the staff man will not consider himself responsible for his decisions, but will fall back on his position as staff, absolving himself from the decision-making responsibility.

Decentralization and Behavior Patterns

The evolution of the computer has given management the ability to process and interpret great masses of information quickly and accurately. The trends toward greater complexity of decision making and to the growth of large organizations have accompanied the development of high-speed computers and sophisticated computer programming. All these factors have led to a major re-evaluation of the centralization-decentralization actions of firms, with the pendulum swinging back toward centralization.

The computer-oriented decisions to recentralize fail to consider the behavioral consequences of such actions. Management's past attempts to use extensive procedure and policy manuals to limit the discretion of the local manager failed for two reasons: first, it was impossible to predict every situation requiring a decision; and second, the local manager became highly dependent and unable to exercise judgment. The more sophisticated programs on third-generation computers certainly have progressed a long way from the old manual approach to management, but it seems that they too can handle only routine decisions.

The manager on the local level finds himself caught between the extremes of apathy, or "I'll do whatever they want," and freedom of action, or "It's my decision and it's going to work." Where he is on the continuum depends on a number of elements. At one extreme is the tendency of the organization to reward, or fail to reward, local initiative. At the other extreme is the motivational pattern of the manager and the question of whether his needs include the right to make decisions on his level. Between these extremes are factors such as the capability of the manager to make local decisions, the attitude of his immediate superior about decentralized decision making, and the magnitude of the decision itself.

The concept of decentralization does not mean that decisions are never made at higher levels. Every employee is subject to some form of control and some form of veto; even the president of the company must answer to the board of directors. Furthermore, the use of a hierarchy in a business firm gives lower levels of management an opportunity to refer a decision to higher levels for action. The well-trained manager will use this hierarchy and will not make decisions which should be made by higher management, even if the decision-making power has been delegated downward through decentralization of the firm's structure.

The informal organization will condition both the decision-making process and the formal organization to meet those personal and institutional needs not satisfied through the highly centralized structure. This was the case in one firm, where a new corporate vice-president of purchasing was appointed to develop a centralized purchasing group that would control purchases previously made by autonomous divisions. The new man sent a letter to the director of purchases in each division explaining his function, asking for cooperation, and requesting that all purchases over $20,000 be cleared with his office.

Every divisional director of purchases responded in writing, noting the need for such a centralized corporate function and indicating his willingness to cooperate. Although numerous purchases of over $20,000 had been made in the past, no such purchases were either consummated or cleared through the corporate purchasing office in the ensuing six months.

The obvious informal action of the divisional directors of purchasing was to ensure that no change occurred in their responsibilities and authorities. Thus, the informal organization was able to condition the formal structure to permit the satisfaction of local needs and conditions.

Until the computer can completely eliminate the human being, management must consider human needs and motivational patterns in designing an organizational structure. A human being is not a robot to be programmed, and if he is programmed, he will usually modify the programming to his own ends. People always have an opportunity to withhold information or perhaps modify it to reflect a more favorable picture of their activities. Furthermore, unless the implementation of the decision is also automated, the individual will modify the implementation as he sees fit. These acts are not sabotage. In most instances, they are conscious attempts to improve the situation and achieve the institutional objectives.

Even when the informal organization is formed to help attain the organizational objectives, it can still run contrary to the best interests of the enterprise. For example, the limited point of view and experience of the lower-level manager can result in the achievement of lower-level objectives at the expense of institutional objectives, even though this optimizing of lower-level objectives is done in all honesty.

Informal organizations also exist at the working level. They often have objectives which run counter to those of the formal organization, since the goal of the informal is personal satisfaction for its members. Through observation and perception, the manager can at least determine the parameters of this social system. He will then be able to predict the effects of his decisions on the workers and to modify them in such a way as to obtain greater acceptance and cooperation. Management builds an informal organization to overcome deficiencies in the formal structure. With the decentralization of authority, management at lower levels receives autonomy, which permits the incorporation of the informal with the formal. Decentralization will not destroy the need for the informal organization, but will merely drive its design lower in the hierarchy.

Decentralization of authority can accomplish many goals:

- It can place the decision where the information is freshest and the implementation fastest.
- It can clear the formal channels of communication and command, permitting greater emphasis on important decisions.

- It can help managers to grow by forcing them to develop judgment, initiative, and decisiveness.
- It can provide recognition, status, and the opportunity for the individual to express his creativity.

But decentralization creates two major problems:

- The exercise of control can destroy decentralization.
- Expertise and the advantage of economy of scale must be provided.

Decentralization creates the appropriate behavioral conditions for the human being to grow and develop. But such growth exacts a price: the control of the organization cannot be as tight, which may result in major errors of human judgment and costly mistakes. Furthermore, decentralization usually requires the utilization of smaller organizations or subparts of organizations, which makes it difficult to develop a high level of specialization or expertise, or to provide the economies of scale which result from large-scale organizations.

Even though these disadvantages are critical and important, on balance decentralization holds greater promise for a company than centralization. In the long run, the effective development of human resources will characterize the more successful organization, and this requires the utilization of decentralized organizational structures. Social systems, informal organizations, and recognition of human development and growth needs greatly affect the manager's leadership methods and styles. The development of the appropriate leadership skills through such understanding will permit the achievement of both the personal goals of organizational members and the institutional goals of the enterprise.

5

The manager operates within the influence of two powerful factors: human behavior, and the dictates of the organizational hierarchy. The latter can either constrain the manager in his dealings with his subordinates, or it can substantially assist him. The environment or climate created by the organizational hierarchy can pervade even the choice of leadership patterns and the exercise of leadership.

Delegation and the Practice of Leadership

THE ORGANIZATIONAL CLIMATE is a composite of many factors, the most important of which are the amount of initiative permitted, the design and operation of a control system, the attitudes of management toward discipline, and what might be called the organizational character. The act of delegation involves all these factors, although the design and operation of a control system may be superimposed on the organizational framework, rather than treated as part of delegation.

Supervision and Delegation

The manager must multiply himself or his activities by coordinating other human beings toward the attainment of a task. To do this, he must order their activities in one of two ways.

The first choice is supervision. Through his superior knowledge and ability, the manager can attempt to anticipate the probable circumstances and problems which will befall his subordinates in carrying through their tasks. He will evolve, implicitly or explicitly, a plan of attack, and will detail the task of the subordinate in carrying through this plan. If exceptions to this plan arise, or if the subordinate is unable to carry it through for any reason, the manager assumes responsibility for taking the requisite action. Little or no initiative is permitted subordinates.

Such supervision is quite appropriate in many industrial situations. If the subordinate is carrying out an unfamiliar task, the manager would probably wish to supervise him. Sometimes the subordinate does not possess the requisite skill; in other situations the manager himself is being supervised by his superior and may not be free to permit his subordinate more discretion than he himself possesses.

The second choice open to the manager in his coordination of subordinates is delegation, which differs drastically from supervision. Delegation consists of granting authority or the right of decision making in certain defined areas, and charging the subordinate with responsibility for carrying through an assigned task. Although the managerial hierarchy of the industrial organization retains the right of veto, that veto should be rarely exercised to overrule the delegated decision.

Delegation is an excellent management method by which to obtain better decisions because of the proximity of lower levels of management to the sources of information. However, regardless of the availability of information and the speed with which decentralized decisions can be made, there is still a major limitation on the efficacy of delegation: the somewhat distorted view which each level of management and each manager holds of the total organization and its objectives. The lower the level of management, the more constrained the point of view and the more potential danger for the total organization. Each manager perceives problems and the decisions relating to those problems from two points of view. The first is his personal frame of reference, which is influenced by his own experiences, attitudes, and the like. This has the greatest influence on his decision. The second is the institutional frame of reference thrust upon him by his position in the managerial hier-

Delegation and the Practice of Leadership 77

archy. But even this frame of reference is colored by the manager's perception of his role in the organization. Figure 5-1 depicts these reference points.

This role perception, coupled with the egocentric tendencies of most men, results in a personal interpretation of a task assignment. The greater the delegation, the greater the danger that these personal factors will influence the manager's decision, and the greater likelihood that his definition of institutional objectives differs from management's definition. The redefinition of institutional objectives and their establishment by lower levels of management may or may not contribute to task attainment. But often the limited frame of reference of the lower levels of management results in subobjectives which at least partially detract from the attainment of organizational objectives. Delegation, then, is not without dangers.

However, delegation also has great strength through its potential for satisfying human needs. When properly practiced, it satisfies the individual both in his search for recognition and in his opportunity for self-determination and self-fulfillment. When the manager delegates work to a subordinate, he says in effect: "I trust you

Figure 5-1
Decision Reference Points

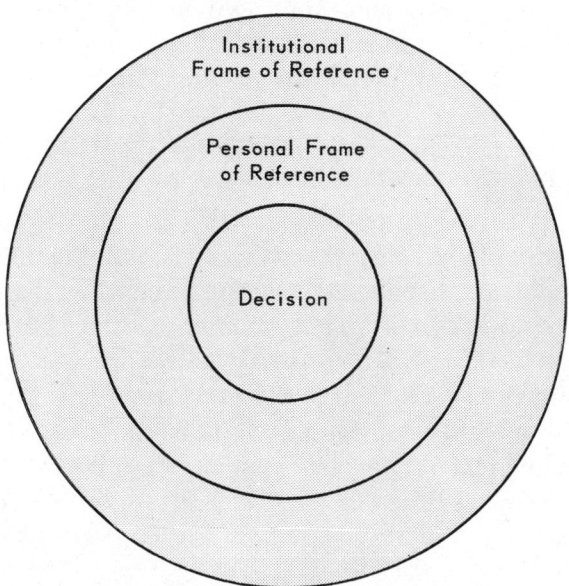

- Institutional Frame of Reference
- Personal Frame of Reference
- Decision

and hereby give you the authority to make decisions." This act of delegation should be announced to other members of the organization so that both the subordinate's peers and those he supervises will be aware of the assignment. In this way, status is conferred on the subordinate and he receives the recognition he desires.

Delegation also permits the individual to achieve the next higher order of need satisfaction: the opportunity for self-fulfillment and self-determination. When delegation is properly utilized, the subordinate knows that he has complete discretion to make decisions. This is true even though the managerial hierarchy demands that each delegated task be the indivisible responsibility of both the delegator and delegatee. The managerial hierarchy also insists that each manager be responsible for all the decisions or actions of his part of the organization, whether or not he delegates any of them to subordinates. This indivisible responsibility is the very cornerstone of organization. But it should serve only to guard against indiscriminate delegation, and not to eliminate the practice of delegation.

Delegation can be one of management's best techniques for satisfying needs and for motivating subordinates to better performance. In terms of the technical aspects of business, delegation through task assignment can achieve faster decisions and eliminate cumbersome information collection systems. In terms of the behavioral aspects, delegation can satisfy man's demands for responsibility, recognition, and the opportunity to exercise initiative.

Delegation and Organizational Needs

Many managerial failures can be attributed to the inability to delegate. At the lowest managerial level, it is possible to supervise a number of employees in a limited situation by dint of hard work, a good memory, and attention to detail. Above-average performance and success in the current job is the major prerequisite for promotion to the next higher managerial position. Little or no analysis is made of how the man attained success, and even if analysis is made, it is rarely correlated to the requirements for promotion. In the higher echelons of the managerial hierarchy, tasks become more complicated, subordinates become more sophisticated, and the demands on time and energy become greater.

Unfortunately, many managers rise to relatively senior positions without understanding the need to change their approach to leadership and to incorporate delegation as a major means of effective leadership. Although attention to detail and a good memory are perhaps critical to success for the first-line supervisor, they are no longer the major requirements for success for the man who is appointed to a higher managerial position. If the newly promoted manager cannot understand his failure to achieve results, he may intensify his attention to detail, which is not applicable to his new position. Soon he is working fourteen to sixteen hours a day, to little or no avail. Eventually he is dismissed, if he does not collapse from exhaustion first.

Delegation is the very heart of organization and a major element of effective leadership. The good delegator recognizes that there are definite physiological and psychological limitations to the ability of any one man to control other men closely. Delegation is not only the means by which the organizational structure provides for the successful assignment and attainment of tasks; it is also a method to facilitate the exercise of leadership through satisfying human needs and motivating subordinates.

Delegation Skills

Each manager evolves his own leadership style and patterns through evaluation both of the business environment and of his own special characteristics. He must be careful to avoid either a routine application of leadership skills or the close emulation of the practices of those he considers successful managers. This is not to say that the manager should not learn from established doctrine in leadership practices and from observation of other managers. The important point is that he must be careful not to use their formulas as panaceas in his search for the solution of leadership problems. Effective leadership practices should be based on an understanding of human behavior, needs, and motivations, rather than on the routine application of some six or seven rules about how to deal with subordinates.

The appropriate utilization of delegation is difficult. Inappropriate and indiscriminate use of delegation can quickly lead to failure. If the manager is unwilling and unable to utilize delegation properly, it is better both for him and the organization that he continue to supervise his subordinates rather than to delegate. The reason for this note of pessimism is that delegation is rarely utilized effectively. One of the greatest dangers of ineffective delegation is the destruction of the relationship between the manager and his subordinates or even of the individual himself as a functioning decision maker. It is fervently recommended that the neophyte manager use the technique of delegation carefully.

The pressures of operating problems and the predilections of the manager often lead to poor delegation practices. Sometimes he is inclined to delegate work which he cannot do himself or does not understand. This is abdication, not delegation. If the manager does not understand any part of an activity for which he is responsible, he is not capable of managing that function. If he is forced into managing a function he does not understand, he must move with all haste to gain a sufficient knowledge of the process or technique so that he will be able to integrate it with his other functions.

The increasing sophistication of management aids such as Operations Research have created uncomfortable situations for the line manager who is beyond his depth in utilizing the fruits of this technique. The increasing need for specialization and heavy utilization of staff often puts the manager in the position of using information which he does not really understand.

This creates difficulties not only for him but also for the newer staff agencies. Operations Research technicians complain bitterly about management's inability to utilize their advanced techniques. They feel thwarted in their attempts to sharpen the information networks and decision-making processes in business. The manager in turn is inclined to avoid using techniques he does not understand, and he rarely feels that he can take the necessary time to learn more about them. He may claim that this knowledge is the responsibility of the specialists he has hired. But they cannot implement their findings and systems without his active cooperation.

The solution to this problem requires two separate but related actions. First, the manager has no alternative but to learn enough about the function so that he can make educated judgments and decisions on the policy-making level. Second, the Operations Research technicians have a responsibility to educate the manager in the use of the function and to present ideas and concepts in nontechnical terms which he will understand. Unfortunately, many technicians want to use jargon to enhance their own status in the company.

In addition, some managers tend to delegate indiscriminately. They work on an intuitive basis, delegating tasks to their subordinates without conducting the necessary preliminary investigations or constructing the detailed plans so essential to effective delegation. Delegation does not consist merely in trusting others; rather, it is a conscious and deliberate action requiring investigation and skill on the part of the manager to determine what and to whom to delegate.

Although this tendency toward indiscriminate delegation often occurs, the more common fault is the failure to delegate. The manager rationalizes that no one can do a job as well as he can. He may be right, but his job is to obtain results through others, and not solely through direct personal action. The fact that the manager can usually, although not always, perform the task better than his subordinates may lead him into trying to do all the work himself.

Every manager has experienced the dire consequences of assigning a task to a subordinate. He found that it took him longer to straighten out the mess left by the subordinate than it would have taken to do the job himself. On one occasion, the subordinate may have failed to follow the correct procedures; on another, his performance of the task may have alienated other managers or other subordinates.

After a few such experiences, the manager may distrust the process of delegation, and do more and more things himself, even down to performing minor details. His workload seems to get heavier every day, as his subordinates ask him more and more questions. The manager starts to come in earlier in the morning and stay later at night to try to find time to handle his managerial responsibilities. He starts to develop a persecution complex, blaming the company and top management for his increasing workload.

Yet if opinions were solicited from the manager's superiors and subordinates, quite a different picture would be painted of the same scene. His superiors would evaluate the manager in terms of his personal output and the performance of his section of the organization. They would indicate that he has fallen short of his performance goals, and that his attitude toward his work makes him hard to get along with. The manager's subordinates would be perhaps even more vehement in their appraisal of the manager, indicating that they can't do anything without seeking his approval first. They would note that his attempts to handle all details have resulted in generally poor performance in all parts of the subsection. Although they may be resigned to the inadequacies of the manager, they usually jump at any chance to be transferred to another part of the company.

This is all too common an occurrence in most organizations. The manager has failed to recognize his leadership task. Instead, he attempts to run a one-man show which usually has but one ending, namely, failure to grow and to receive promotion. The basic premise of organization and of management is that the sum of the group action is greater than the sum of the individual actions. The major key to effective group action is delegation. Until the manager learns to delegate, effective group action is well nigh impossible.

Delegation and Planning

Delegation at first sight seems to be one of the simplest of leadership techniques. But the widespread failure of managers to practice effective delegation soon casts doubt on this conclusion. Effective delegation is like any other effective managerial action in that it requires careful planning. When the manager evolves a plan, he must also determine how it is to be implemented and carried through. A major problem, both in the plan and its implementation, is the assignment of its parts or tasks to subordinates. At this point, the manager must determine which tasks are to be delegated, and to whom.

Delegation must be done not only in accord with a plan; it must also be done in accord with the organizational structure and its parts. The original design of that structure, although a compromise, was based on the premise that there would be effective delegation and implementation of plans at all levels of management. If the organizational structure is well designed, it will set the stage for the assignment of tasks and the delegation of authority and responsibility.

However, the original organizational structure, no matter how well planned, is modified over time, often unofficially, through delegation which did not fit within the structure. The exigencies of the moment may lead the manager into acts of delegation which are not in accord with the accepted organizational structure. A case can be made for such assignments even when they run contrary to the normal practices of the firm—but they must not be made indiscriminately. They must be part of the plan of attack evolved by the manager to solve problems, and the long-run consequences of such delegation on the organizational structure must be carefully considered. It may even be necessary to amend the structure to agree with newly planned delegation.

Delegation without consideration of the needs of the organization or of its members does occur, and may lead to uneven workloads. This fact is not the major criticism of such a practice. Rather, the problem is one of implementing plans and decisions.

All organizations evolve a system akin to social systems. Certain people are assigned certain tasks, not necessarily through the formal hierarchy of management, but rather through the day-to-day evolution of practices. As long as people work within this system, they will usually receive cooperation and assistance. But when a new situation is thrust upon this social system, there is a danger of rejection.

When the assignment of a function is normally made to a particular individual, a change in this practice may meet great resistance in the system. Because this system has become the de facto organizational structure, the manager must take it into account in his practice of delegation. If he does not, the newly assigned subordinate will have great difficulty carrying through his delegated assignment. It is possible for the manager to run counter to the system, but in doing so he must be willing to accept the consequences of his actions.

Leadership Skills in Delegation

There is yet another prerequisite for effective delegation. The manager must evaluate the capabilities of his subordinate to carry through the delegated task. If the manager has any doubts about those capabilities, he must take the route of supervision rather than delegation. There is a place for both in leadership practices. Supervision is an excellent method for teaching methods and procedures to subordinates. By utilizing supervision first, the manager can evaluate the ability of the subordinate to carry through delegated tasks. But until the manager is sure of his subordinate's capabilities, he should not utilize delegation.

Why must the manager be so careful in utilizing delegation? The answer lies in the differentiation between delegation and supervision. Supervision accepts and admits the need for constant checking on the subordinate's performance. Its basic premise is that he has not yet reached the point of sophistication where he no longer needs frequent help and assistance. The manager, as the supervisor, is a teacher who is constantly involved in the instruction of his subordinates. In contrast, when he delegates a task, he gives his subordinate complete power, authority, and responsibility to carry out that function. Once the assignment is made, the manager is no longer involved directly in its definition or solution. He has given the subordinate the decision-making power over this particular function. Unlike supervision, delegation does not give the manager the right to check on his subordinate's every action.

The difference between supervision and delegation can be quite subtle. A hypothetical case might serve at this point to differentiate these two practices. The assumption is made that the necessary conditions prerequisite to effective delegation have been fulfilled. The delegation is being made according to a plan, in accord with the dictates of the organizational structure, and in full recognition of the capabilities of the subordinate to carry through the delegated task. The manager calls in his subordinate and sets forth the conditions and details of the assignment. Their communication is effective, so that no doubts exist in the mind of either party about the assigned task. At this point, the manager indicates to the subordinate that the latter has full authority and responsibility to carry through his assignment.

After a few days elapse, the subordinate comes in to discuss his assignment with the manager. He outlines three alternatives, A, B, and C, and then asks the manager which he should choose. The manager, cognizant of the concept of delegation and of the need to develop his subordinate to make his own decisions, counters the query by asking what course of action the subordinate would choose. Meanwhile, the manager evaluates the alternatives in his mind, and concludes that the only successful one would be C. But the subordinate answers the manager by saying that he would choose alternative A. The manager had silently considered A to be the worst of the three alternatives.

The manager is now in a serious dilemma. If he questions the choice of the subordinate in any way, the subordinate will be inclined to rescind his own decision and search for the decision required by the manager. This will set up unsatisfactory behavior patterns, because the subordinate will lose confidence in his own ability to make decisions and in the manager's willingness to permit him to do so. Yet if the manager allows the subordinate to follow what he considers to be an unsatisfactory solution to the problem, there may be dire consequences for the company, the subordinate, and the manager.

Undoubtedly, at this point the manager recognizes that he has made at least two errors. The first error was to trust the subordinate to make the decision in the first place, since he was apparently not capable of doing so. The second error was not to discuss the alternatives in greater detail with the subordinate before he asked for a decision. He should have pointed out the advantages and disadvantages of each choice so that the subordinate could reach a better decision. But once the subordinate has made the decision, any action by the manager would seem to be a veto of the delegation.

At this juncture the manager faces a difficult decision. He either rescinds the delegation, with dire consequences for the relationship between himself and his subordinate, or he permits the subordinate to carry through a decision that the manager considers unsatisfactory. The critical point is that if the manager fails to let the subordinate carry through alternative A, he has failed to delegate.

Delegation can be an effective tool. If it is used improperly or indiscriminately, it can destroy the effectiveness of an organization, because control will become a major problem. The lack of careful planning for delegation creates considerable doubt as to whether a task will be performed according to plan. Under these conditions the manager will have difficulty in coordination.

Another major danger of the improper use of delegation is the failure to develop initiative and decisiveness in subordinates. Both the manager and his subordinate must have a clear idea of what is involved in delegation. Most people think they want responsibility, but in practice they are inclined to avoid it. The right to make a decision carries with it accountability for that decision. Within most business organizations, responsibility is rarely assigned lightly. The chances are that a man to whom a task is delegated for the first time will not previously have been responsible for decisions or personal actions in the firm. Therefore, his first experience with delegation is traumatic. But it is traumatic for the manager, too, because he will have great doubts and worries about whether the task will be carried through successfully. The subordinate tends to want to pass the delegated task back to the manager, and the manager tends to want to resume responsibility. Both must resist these instincts if delegation is to be practiced.

Leadership Responsibilities in Delegation

Effective delegation requires planning, correlation with the organizational structure, and preliminary evaluation of the subordinate's ability to carry through the delegated task. These first steps, although essential, will not alone result in effective delegation. The manager must also coordinate the delegation with his subordinate. The act of delegation does not include abdication of responsibilities by the manager. Not only must he perform the necessary preliminary steps before considering delegation, but he must also fulfill certain responsibilities to his subordinates during the process of delegation.

Although the manager wishes to use delegation as a means to divorce himself from performing certain tasks, he still must coordinate this delegated task with his total job. He undoubtedly has some definite ideas on what he wishes his subordinate to achieve

Establish Checkpoints. The distinction between supervision and delegation has been made repeatedly in this chapter. Delegation has been defined as the act of giving complete power, authority, and responsibility to the subordinate to carry out a function. But the experienced manager could argue that no one has such power, no matter what his position in the firm. This point cannot be denied. There must be operation of controls over all parts of the organization. It is not, then, a question of whether a manager will relinquish his control over his subordinate through delegation, but of how this control is to be exercised.

A delegated task is usually sufficiently important and lengthy in application so that the subordinate will be expected to evolve a plan for its achievement. Such a plan should go through the standard process of being related to higher plans in the organization, which will automatically provide an element of control. In addition, the subordinate will be responsible not only for planning but also for establishing the controls which will be exercised to insure that the plan, and therefore the delegated task, is carried out successfully. The establishment of these controls by the subordinate should be a requirement of delegation, although the manager will have some input into determining them. In order to gain maximum advantage from the personal relationship between the manager and the subordinate, these controls should be set up as automatic checkpoints calling for either reports or conferences to evaluate progress. Any dialog with the manager is either initiated by the subordinate or called for automatically by the system. There is no interference by the manager.

When the manager utilizes supervision, he initiates the control system and the evaluation of the performance of his subordinate. When delegation is used, such controls and evaluations are initiated by the subordinate as part of the total plan for the carrying through the delegated task.

Evaluate and Review. The responsibility for evaluation and review must rest with the manager more heavily than with the subordinate. Business has wholeheartedly adopted the old adage of learning by doing, as evidenced by the accent in business on the need for experience. But experience, like any other teacher, can be effective only if the person being taught makes the necessary effort to learn. All too frequently the same mistake is repeated time after

Delegation and the Practice of Leadership

in handling of the assigned task. The subordinate must
parameters of the task and how it fits into the total plans t
the objectives of the firm. An additional requirement is
some system or method which will enable both the man
the subordinate to know that the delegated task is pi
satisfactorily. Finally, there must be a process of evaluatioi
punitive reasons but as an integral part of the personal dev(
of both the manager and the subordinate.

There are four distinct steps in the delegation process
preliminary investigation of whether the task should be d(

Provide Direction. The manager is responsible for p
direction and leadership to his subordinates. He must mal
able his vast experience and judgment to the subordinate
destroying the latter's discretionary delegated powers of
making. This direction and the benefit of the manager's exp
should be provided at the time of delegation. In the illu
given earlier in this chapter, the manager failed to provi
direction, with disastrous results. Some managers feel that e)
briefing amounts to supervision rather than delegation, ar
the best test of a man's ability is to give him the job and let
it. But this line of reasoning would negate the whole pro
education, which has a place in the firm. The major point
such instruction should be a preliminary to the process of dele
and not a veto of decisions already made by the subordinate.

Set Up Guideposts. The term "policy" might very well b
stituted for "guideposts." The manager must give answers to
tions such as: What are the limits of the subordinate's auth
What resources are to be made available to the subordinate to p
him to carry through the assigned task? What relationship
this assigned task bear to the total task of the organization?

Ideally, the manager should have thought through the an
to these questions prior to delegating the task. But these que:
may involve the manager in too detailed an investigation. An
native method would be to delegate the assignment with the p
sion that the subordinate has time to conduct a preliminar
vestigation to determine what he needs to carry out the task.
method has the advantage of giving the manager some insight
the subordinate's thought processes and capabilities prior to
delegation.

time in business. The pressure for action leaves the manager little time to analyze his past errors in order to avoid repeating them. Only through conscious evaluation can future mistakes be prevented. Periodic performance evaluation of employees is a step in the right direction, but it is no substitute for a detailed and introspective evaluation by the manager of his own performance in delegation.

The manager often tends to use the evaluation for grading or rating subordinates rather than for contributing to their development. The process of delegation places a subordinate in a position to test his own ideas and abilities. Although there are undoubtedly constraints on the subordinate's actions and many difficulties in the way of his implementation of his plans, the manager has nevertheless done everything in his power to permit the subordinate to make his own decisions. Prompt and effective evaluation and review will teach the subordinate a great deal in a very short time because of his personal involvement in the task.

However, such a review and evaluation should be designed as part of the total plan of attack for the achievement of the delegated task. The control system should be designed to generate information which will provide a concrete basis for the review. In this way, the evaluation and review will be a learning process rather than a punitive experience. The accent must be on how a job could have been performed better, not on who was responsible for the errors. This positive attitude should benefit both the manager and the subordinate. The manager will be in a position to make subsequent delegations more effective, and the subordinate will be better able to carry out such delegated tasks.

Common Faults in Delegation

To be more effective in delegation, the manager should examine critically his own delegation practices. Following are the four major faults in delegation. They are presented in detail to aid the manager in evaluating his own delegation practices.

Too Close Supervision. Although a differentiation has been made between supervision and delegation, it is difficult in practice to draw the line so finely. If the manager leans too heavily toward supervision although ostensibly practicing delegation, he will fail to gather the fruits of either. For the subordinate to gain the full satisfaction possible from delegation, he must complete *all* stages in achieving the delegated task. First, he must recognize the problem; second, he must be forced to consider alternative solutions; third, he must decide on one of the solutions; and fourth, he must implement his solution. The manager must permit his subordinate to go through these four steps *without* interference, or the subordinate will be frustrated emotionally in his fulfillment of the task. Frustration can lead to many actions, but the most probable in business is either aggression or apathy. If the subordinate becomes aggressive, he will reject the manager even to the point of leaving the firm. Apathy in many ways is far worse, since it may result in the destruction of the subordinate as a potentially successful manager.

Failure to Provide Direction. The manager who truly understands the process of delegation is inclined more toward offering too little direction than toward too much. He tends to lean over backward to give the subordinate every opportunity to exercise discretion and decision-making power. In some instances, the result of this overzealous approach to delegation is that the subordinate does not know what is expected of him. The manager wants to give his subordinate every opportunity to grow, but such growth must be planned and directed. No man can be a completely free agent in an organization if objectives are to be attained. Through the promulgation of objectives and the establishment of policies, the organization attempts to set forth the direction for its members to follow. The individual manager has no less responsibility toward his subordinates. He must provide direction for the delegation by establishing the constraints of authority and responsibility and offering any pertinent information he possesses.

Again, the difficulty facing the manager is to distinguish between delegation and supervision. In delegation, the manager directs his subordinate, not by interference, but by evaluation of results.

Managers must constantly make decisions on whether to accomplish a task through supervision or delegation. For example, if the manager in the area of inventory control plans to go the route of supervision, he may evolve a formula to determine the number of individual units to be maintained in inventory. He assigns a subordinate the task of making such calculations, with the understanding that any situations not covered by the rules determined by the manager should be referred to him for decision. The manager feels free to make his own checks on inventory and on the calculations made by his subordinate. There is no pretense that this procedure in any way involves delegation.

On the other hand, if the manager wishes to delegate the task of inventory control to his subordinate, he sets forth the general parameters of the problem. He might indicate what the total amount of the dollar value of inventory should be, and the minimum amount of inventory needed in order to avoid work stoppages. If the manager feels that some types of solutions are not applicable to this problem, he indicates these limitations to his subordinate. (Of course, he will have evaluated the latter's competence to carry out the delegated task before issuing instructions.) It is now the responsibility of the subordinate to determine how to meet the objectives of maintaining an adequate level of inventory within certain dollar limitations. Although he is encouraged to discuss the technical aspects of the job with the manager, the decisions on inventory control are left to the subordinate.

An important part of the subordinate's plan for the inventory control system is how to report his performance to the manager. He can do this in many different ways, but certainly the overall figures of the total investment in inventory can serve as one of the control measures provided by the manager. If this investment exceeds the budgeted figure, the subordinate takes the necessary action to correct the deviations. But if such corrections do not take place, it is the manager's responsibility to discuss the matter with the subordinate so that the latter can indicate what measures he will take to correct the deviation.

This situation represents control by results, not control by interference. The manager does not interfere with the subordinate's performance of the delegated task. He does not ask to look at the subordinate's calculations. But neither does he abdicate his responsibility to provide direction to the subordinate.

There cannot be hard and fast rules to govern delegation practices. Rather, the manager must develop his own rules of thumb on when to use supervision and when to use delegation. What is direction by one man would become interference by another. It is more the attitude of the manager toward delegation which counts. Such an attitude will be a direct product of the manager's understanding of the process of delegation.

Lack of Accountability. One of the greatest weaknesses of many managers is their failure to check on the performance of a delegated task. This soon creates a sense of irresponsibility which quickly spreads to all parts of the organization. This concept of accountability is directly related to the satisfaction of human needs. A strong need, certainly for managers and for those striving to become managers, is that of recognition. If a man is held accountable for his performance of a delegated task, satisfactory performance automatically leads to recognition. But if such recognition is to be an effective motivator, it must have value in the status system of the firm. If unsatisfactory performance is permitted without retribution, then recognition for a job well done becomes an empty thing. The result may be that recognition of the accomplishment of a delegated task will fail to motivate individuals in the organization. This will in turn lead them to turn their attention to the satisfaction of some other need or to attain recognition through another channel. Accountability becomes not a matter of discipline but an effective means of motivation within the firm.

Usurping Authority. Many managers who apparently practice delegation usurp the very authority they have delegated. This tendency is difficult to overcome. When they see a subordinate apparently failing to carry through his delegated task successfully, their reaction is to jump in and solve the problem. They will always rationalize this action by noting to themselves that a mistake would be costly for them personally or for the firm. But such action invalidates the theory of delegation. Delegation may be costly in terms of the mistakes made by those delegated responsibilities, but it is the manager's responsibility *before* delegation to determine whether he and the company can afford a mistake in the delegated task. If the potential costs of the mistake are too high, either the manager must assume the responsibility himself, or must find someone who is capable of carrying through the delegated task. He should not usurp the delegated authority once the delegation is made.

Delegation can be a great builder of capable management. Through the judicious and selective use of delegation, a program of executive development through practical experience can be instituted. But such executive development has a price—the potential and probable mistakes resulting directly from the practice of delegation.

Evaluation and Counseling

Inherent in the task of leadership is the development of subordinates. Although the manager is forced to be action oriented on a short-range basis, his success is really determined by what he builds for the future. Du Pont even states that its real product is its management. But management is a product of management. Whatever the innate ability of the manager, and whatever college education and specialized courses he had had, he can gain true insight into the practice of management and leadership only through actual work experience and the constant evaluation and counseling he receives from the next higher level of management.

Effective evaluation, although aided by personnel devices such as merit rating and performance evaluation forms, cannot be a mechanical process performed at periodic intervals required by personnel policies. Rather, it is a constantly recurring process. The manager must never let slip by the opportunity to evaluate and improve his own performance and that of his subordinates. This identification of weaknesses and strengths can greatly aid him in developing managerial capabilities.

Inextricably tied up with the process of evaluation is counseling. Evaluation is only the means to the end of counseling, which will result in the development of the individual. There is little doubt that in every company, managers are charged, explicitly or implicitly, with the responsibility of developing their subordinates. Management development can be greatly assisted by the use of practices such as delegation and job assignment, but it is only through counseling that the fruits of these practices can be garnered.

Some people develop the necessary insights without counseling. By training themselves to practice objectivity and a high degree of perception, they can identify their own weaknesses and strengths. But such people are more the exception than the rule. Normally counseling is necessary to identify those areas and to set forth a plan of action to reinforce the strengths and eliminate or minimize the weaknesses.

No one will deny that counseling is an integral part of the manager's job. One survey conducted by the author indicated that 76.9 percent of the responding firms explicitly charged management with the responsibility for coaching and counseling subordinates.[1] But for some reason, top management has never adequately recognized the magnitude and difficulty of the task. Counselors in the educational system require extensive university training, usually including a thorough knowledge of psychology and sociology as well as specialized courses and work in counseling. The psychological journals are replete with articles on the intricacies of counseling and its ancillary functions.

Where does the man suddenly promoted to management ranks acquire this specialized ability to counsel and coach others? Top management in particular and industry in general have been remiss in training managers in this all-important function. Perhaps it would behoove industry to pay as much attention to training its managers in effective counseling methods as it has paid to applied human relations.

A basic tenet of management is that each employee has only one superior or boss. The introduction of the staff concept has officially permitted each man access to more people in the organization than only his one boss, but this has not invalidated the basic tenet. Just as Moses broke the Host of Israel into thousands, hundreds, and tens, so does the modern organization assign its members a position and a superior. To insure that the organizational structure will not break down, the reporting of one man to one boss, or the unity of command, as it is commonly labeled, is basic.

The organization also sets forth channels of communication based upon this formalization of the organizational structure. Although certain other formal channels of communication are open to the individual employee, such as his union or the personnel department, in practice his future, his work effectiveness, and his personal satisfaction are in the hands of his superior.

[1] Douglas C. Basil, *Executive Development: A Comparison of Large and Small Enterprise* (Minneapolis, Minnesota: University of Minnesota, School of Business Administration, 1964), p. 36, prepared for the Small Business Administration, Washington, D.C., 1964.

This hierarchical system places a heavy weight indeed on the manager in his counseling of subordinates. On the one hand, he is charged by the organization with the responsibility for task accomplishment through the development of the human resources allocated to him. On the other hand, he is responsible for the personal development and future of his subordinates, who have no other avenue for such development within their present organization. Obviously, the manager cannot take such a responsibility lightly. But at the present stage of managerial development in most industrial organizations, the manager must develop this counseling capability himself.

The first stage in the development of counseling skills is a more thorough understanding of human behavior. The manager must learn to deal with emotional as well as rational problems. But evaluation and counseling are fraught with the perils of human nature and human behavior, and objectivity is a difficult trait to develop. It is man's nature to be subjective, thrusting human and personal factors to the fore. Although the manager may decry this lack of objectivity on the part of his subordinates, he should be realistic in recognizing that all human beings are subjective to some extent, including himself. But the process of evaluation attempts to strip subjectivity from the individual. Necessarily, evaluation must be impersonal, objective, and factual. The dilemma for the manager is how to make an objective evaluation when there are so many subjective overtones.

The manager must recognize that it is the nature of man to react against frustration and relieve his tensions by aggression, sublimation, or other behavior. He must understand that rationalization is one of the ways the human mind can adjust to the inadequacies of the human being. He must recognize the importance of identifying his subordinates' needs and utilizing these needs to motivate them to better performance. These factors and countless others must be included in the inventory of knowledge of the effective manager.

Through such an understanding of human behavior, the manager will recognize that evaluation and counseling are complex and difficult tasks. They raise specters in the mind of the man being evaluated; he may see them as threats to his security, as an injustice, and even as the failure of the manager to understand the situation. To use the process of evaluation effectively, the manager must establish rapport with his subordinate. The latter must recognize that the manager is motivated by a wish to develop him as a more effective performer. This wish does not have to be considered altruistic. It is quite in order for the manager to indicate to his subordinate that such development is in the best interest of both of them. But it is still in this area that the manager will have his greatest difficulty in providing the necessary leadership to develop his subordinates both individually and as members of a team. It is also in this area that the manager can make one of his greatest contributions to the organization and to his subordinates.

Leadership and Delegation in Review

An established management technique—delegation—can afford the manager ample opportunity to exercise good leadership practices. Like any other tool, delegation must be used properly to obtain results. Delegation is not only a management technique but also a leadership technique. The subordinate may require recognition or even self-fulfillment, which can be satisfied by the proper practice of delegation. But dangers lie in improper use of delegation. Delegation permits the individual freedom of action within certain well-defined limits. Interference with the delegated task by the manager can result in a series of behavior problems ranging from aggression to apathy. Therefore, delegation is not something to be used indiscriminately.

There is a distinct difference between supervision, which allows the subordinate little or no decision-making powers, and delegation, which assigns very definite decision-making powers. There is a place for supervision with the untried employee, just as there is a place for delegation when it is used properly. Certain prerequisites to delegation must be observed if delegation is to be effective: (1) the delegation should conform to the organizational structure; (2) the subordinate must be judged capable of satisfactory completion of the task; and (3) the delegation must be done in accord with some overall plan for completion of the task.

Once the delegation has been made, the manager must accept the decisions of his subordinate if they fall within the previously prescribed limits. There is a great tendency for the manager to overrule his subordinate's decisions. If he does so, delegation ceases, and the relationship between superior and subordinate deteriorates.

Delegation can help subordinates develop into better managers. But the manager still has a responsibility, over and above the act of delegation, to assist this development by evaluation and counseling. The objective of counseling is the development of better management practices by both the manager and his subordinate. The atmosphere must be one of joint development and learning, not of chastisement.

6

Control is all pervasive, both in the business firm and in society at large. Control is one of the integral tasks of the manager; without it, the setting of objectives, the structuring of an organization, the exercise of leadership, and the development of plans are not effective. And because controls restrict the freedom of action of the individual, they have serious behavioral implications.

Behavioral Patterns in Management Controls

CONTROLS POSE a threat to the security of the individual. To most persons, "control" connotes "evaluation," which runs counter to the elaborate defense mechanisms every human being develops to permit him to live with reality. Furthermore, rarely is evaluation solely for private consumption. Its results quickly become known throughout the organization and can not only disturb the equilibrium of the individual, but can also tend to impair his status in the organization.

In the nonhuman, mechanistic world of management processes and practices, control by means of a comparison of actual against planned performance seems coldly logical and realistic. A budget is set, deviations from it are noted, and corrective action is taken. It would seem that nothing could be simpler. In reality, nothing could be more complex.

The effect of that complexity on human behavior is well illustrated by the experience of a capable M.B.A. graduate who attempted to apply his education and business experience to his job. He was hired from a competitor to be the regional sales manager in a firm which had elaborate standards of performance. Information was collected on sales by region, product, salesman, ratio of salesman's expense to his sales, and so on. The bright young man decided that he would attempt to apply the management practices he had learned in school. One of the first tasks he undertook was an examination of his region in terms of factors such as economic conditions, per capita disposable income, and penetration of the market by his product and those of his competitors. On the basis of this and other investigations, he constructed a long-range plan of action to gain a larger share of the market, and concurrently to reduce sales costs as a percentage of the sales dollar.

To achieve these objectives, he decided it was necessary to eliminate certain marginal accounts and to concentrate on developing new accounts with greater potential. He communicated his ideas to the general sales manager, who cautioned him to make sure that he would still meet his quotas. The regional sales manager argued that in the short run he might not be able to meet his quotas, because it would take time to establish these new accounts. He was again warned and admonished that it was up to him to run his own show.

After much soul-searching, the regional sales manager decided that his plan would be in the best interests of his region and therefore of the company. When the quarterly sales statistics were released, he was told that he was falling behind his quotas and should get on the ball. When the annual review of sales statistics was made, sales volume had in fact fallen more than 20 percent, although sales expenses had also been reduced by about 10 percent. The regional sales manager was called on the carpet and severely chastised for his failure to achieve his sales quotas. It was made abundantly clear to him that further failure of this sort would result in dismissal.

The regional sales manager became embittered against the company. His own analysis had indicated that his strategy of cultivating new accounts was just beginning to pay dividends. New accounts constituted well over 30 percent of his total sales. His elimination of marginal accounts had in fact decreased his sales expenses by over 30 percent, although he had to reinvest two-thirds of this saving in the cultivation of new accounts. His calculations showed that by the end of the following year he would reach his existing quotas, and that at the end of five years he would double them. But he knew that if he continued to follow this policy, he would be unable to adhere to the control standards set forth for his region and would be relieved of his position. He was in a dilemma.

He tried every possible line of attack to obtain permission to follow through his plan. He failed at every turn. His reaction could easily have been forecast by any psychologist: Unresolved frustration will lead to a change in behavior pattern. He decided if that was the way the company wanted to run the sales department, it was fine with him. If he could not beat them, he would join them. He returned to his region and reinstituted the old emphasis on immediate sales volume. Because of his personal superiority, he was easily able to beat the system and turn in sales volumes which easily exceeded the quota.

Longer range, there were two disastrous consequences of this control system. The first was that the company lost because its control system emphasized adherence to outmoded standards which were essentially short run in operation. The second consequence was far more serious. The control system destroyed the initiative and motivation of one of the company's finest young managers. This had serious consequences not only for the firm, which sacrificed managerial talent, but also for the manager, who no longer had any outlet for his creative abilities.

Obviously, in this illustration the control system did change the manager's pattern of behavior. Unfortunately, the end result of that change was not the attainment of objectives but rather adherence to standards. The autocratic nature of the firm, coupled with the control system's accent on adherence to narrow standards, can create many mutations of human behavior.

Conformity and Social Patterns

The accent of the organization man is on conformity to patterns of behavior established for the executive class by the firm. Much of this conformity is sociological in nature, stressing personality conformity. How did this state of affairs develop? It is doubtful that a special managerial sociological class was created with its own taboos, mores, and customs which transcended individual organizations. It is more likely that such personality conformity grew out of the control systems and the standards of performance established by the firm.

The student who was in college before the 1960s was expected to represent a particular stratum of society which would be superior to other strata and inferior to strata such as graduate students or an executive class. But within his own group, the exceptional student was not tolerated. The student who was overeager or generally performed well above average was rejected by the group. This was the era of the gentleman C grade.

In the 1960s, a subtle but important change of emphasis—from mediocrity to excellence—took place in the social structure. The high school student realized that he had to produce exceptional work if he was to be admitted to the college of his choice. The same motivation applied to his undergraduate work, because of the increasing need to take graduate study to gain professional competence. It will be interesting to observe what will happen in the ranks of executives in the 1970s as a result of this emphasis on superior performance for today's graduate and undergraduate students.

As greater emphasis is placed on controls in decentralized operation, there will be an increasing tendency toward insisting that the organization man adapt his behavior to the system, unless a shift occurs in the current philosophies of control. Another behavior pattern directly attributable to controls is what is often called the civil service mind. The emphasis on conformity to rigid standards of performance, as set forth in written policy manuals and rules and regulations, creates a situation where the individual will not exercise initiative. If he cannot find an answer to a question in the firm's rule book, his reply will be, "It's against company policy."

The civil service mind is more frequently found in larger organizations where bureaucracy has taken firmer root. Obviously, the civil service concept is rampant in government at both local and national levels. The concentration of national resources in relatively few large firms may have disastrous results if the civil service concept becomes as widespread in industry as it is in government. In fact, there is some question whether the United States can retain world industrial leadership unless management becomes more daring and more willing to take risks.

It is interesting that one of the most significant changes in the structure of American management during the past half-century—the major shift from owner-managers to professional managers—may have sown the seeds of future discord. That change has not only brought an end to nepotism, but has also increased the emphasis on professional training and competence, and led to a greater devotion to the cause of more effective management. But it has also heralded the end of entrepreneurship, with its accent on innovation and risk-taking.

The separation of ownership and management, coupled with the widespread distribution of ownership through the sale of shares in stock exchanges, has created a strange phenomenon: the stockholder's lack of interest in appraising the acts of the professional manager. Essentially the stockholder is content as long as the company makes a satisfactory profit for paying dividends and the price of the stock appreciates over time in the stock market.

This situation forces the professional manager into somewhat the same behavior pattern forced on the lower levels of management: He must consider the short term as more important than the long term. He is rewarded essentially for not rocking the boat. If he undertook a venture which endangered short-run profits, even though the result would be large long-term gain, he might be unable to fulfill his plans because of the stockholder's demand for short-term results.

The entrepreneur is rewarded in full by profit for his risk. In contrast, the professional manager receives a salary, albeit a high salary, which does not necessarily reflect the effect of high profits. Thus, he has much less incentive to take great risks, except possibly for the exercise of stock options, or profit-activated bonuses. This difference in motivation points to an increase in the number of people with the civil service mind even at the top management level in American industry.

Some of the major errors made by subsidiaries or divisions of larger corporations in the past decade have sounded the death knell of greater decentralization of organizational structure and authority.

If anything, the trend will be toward greater centralization, even with its attendant disadvantages. But perhaps the greatest disadvantage of centralization is not well enough recognized by top management. The manager's desire to exercise initiative is related to more than ego satisfaction. Decisions can be made best when information is available to use in making the decision and when quick and decisive action can be taken. Much of the answer to this problem lies in the design and the operation of control systems.

Motivation and Control

Another potential behavior pattern resulting from the operation of control systems is an antimanagement or anticompany feeling. For a long time there has been a divergence of interests and objectives between management and labor. Each side distrusts and misunderstands the other. Management often takes the position that the worker is inherently lazy and must be closely controlled to achieve any satisfactory standard of productivity. Labor, for its part, believes that management wants to exploit the worker and is inherently antihuman and too profit oriented. This difference of opinion is not solely a matter of semantics or of ineffective communication. It is more a matter of management practices.

Douglas McGregor examined the motivational factors underlying control in his epoch-making book, *The Human Side of Enterprise*.[1] He stated that there are three basic tenets inherent in Theory X, or the traditional view of control:

1. The average human being has an inherent dislike of work and will avoid it if he can.

2. Because of this human characteristic, most people must be coerced, controlled, directed, or threatened with punishment to get them to put forth adequate effort toward the achievement of organizational objectives.

3. The average human being prefers to be directed, wishes to avoid responsibility, has relatively little ambition, and wants security above all.

[1] Douglas McGregor, *The Human Side of Enterprise* (New York: McGraw-Hill Book Company, 1960).

McGregor thought that Theory X is outmoded and inadequate for management today. He advocated replacing it with a new Theory Y, which would integrate goals with the following basic tenets:

1. The expenditure of physical and mental effort in work is as natural as play or rest. The average human being does not inherently dislike work. Depending upon controllable conditions, work may be a source of satisfaction (and will be voluntarily performed) or a source of punishment (and will be avoided if possible).

2. External control, or threat of punishment, is not the only means of bringing about effort toward organizational objectives. Man will exercise self-direction and self-control in the service of objectives to which he is committed.

3. Commitment to objectives is a function of the rewards associated with their achievement. The most significant of such rewards—the satisfaction of ego and other needs—can be direct products of effort directed toward organizational objectives.

4. Under proper conditions, the average human being learns not only to accept but to seek responsibility. Avoidance of responsibility, lack of ambition, and emphasis on security are generally consequences of experience, not inherent human characteristics.

5. The capacity to exercise a relatively high degree of imagination, ingenuity, and creativity in the solution of organizational problems is widely, not narrowly, distributed in the population.

6. Under the conditions of modern industrial life, the intellectual potentialities of the average human being are only partially utilized.[2]

These concepts are currently receiving a great deal of attention from practicing management.[3] The emphasis now is on understanding and utilizing motivation. Yet it is not enough to improve the interpersonal relationships between management and workers or manager and manager. The formal system of organization is still the framework within which work will be performed. Regardless of the strength of the informal organization, the overall impact of the

---

[2] Ibid., pp. 47–48.

[3] Douglas McGregor, *The Professional Manager*, edited by Caroline McGregor and Warren G. Bennis (New York: McGraw-Hill Book Company, 1967). In this book, published posthumously, Professor McGregor related his Theories X and Y to managerial philosophy, rather than to control per se.

formal organization will still leave its mark on the behavior of individual members. Until this new philosophy permeates the formal organizational structure, it will be most difficult for the manager to combat this anticompany feeling.

A control system which exists solely to police managers and workers fails to take into account the findings of the behavioral sciences on motivation, and ignores the social revolution taking place all over the world today. Younger people are demanding greater challenge and opportunity. They are questioning the very institutions of Western society. The individual is no longer submissive. The young man of today expects more from his job and from his company, in terms not only of salary and fringe benefits but also of opportunity. He is far better educated and prepared for life than his father or his grandfather. He craves responsibility, he wants to exercise initiative, and he begs for the chance to be creative.

The majority of young people today are neither delinquent nor lazy. They want to live a full life and to contribute to society. Their demands offer great challenges to management. By creating the proper climate for work, the manager can motivate his employees. At this point, the manager of the old school may say that it is the responsibility of the individual to motivate himself, to be a self-starter. He was raised without being motivated by his superiors, and can see no reason why he should be forced to motivate others.

However, the social revolution has established one most important point: This new breed of educated man will demand superior performance from the manager. No longer will the manager be able to merely command. He will have to make his subordinates understand and participate in the task so that they will be motivated to assist him in accomplishing it. This point deserves great emphasis. The action of any manager will create behavior patterns among those affected by his actions. If he is to be an effective manager, he must insure that his actions create the appropriate behavior patterns.

All too often a control system results in the removal of the opportunity for initiative in decision making at lower levels of management, although the objective may have been to remove the possibility of major errors in judgment. To accomplish that objective, the control system may operate within very narrow bounds; in other words, standards of performance are set in such a way that the manager has no alternative but to conform to those standards. Because no human mind can anticipate all possible situations, such stringent controls cannot handle every situation.

This emphasis on conformity to rigid standards may condition the manager to make irrational decisions. This happened to the manager of a branch of a firm selling specialty articles to retailers. He faced a difficult dilemma in his investment in inventory. The firm had definitely established standards of stock turn (the number of times the stock was sold and reordered in a year), and of return on investment in inventory.

A new firm opened a branch in the city and decided that the best way to compete was on the basis of service. The new firm stocked items whose turnover was limited, so that its salesmen could boast to customers that the firm gave immediate delivery on hard-to-get items. In addition, the new firm carried a much larger inventory of commonly stocked items, permitting the immediate shipment of large orders.

The manager of the older firm knew that he would be held strictly accountable for his stock turn and return of investment on inventory figures. He knew that if he owned his own business, he would undoubtedly take immediate action to increase inventory in order to meet competition. But his firm's strict control system gave him so little leeway in exercising initiative that he could take no action to counter the moves of his competition. The result of his inability to increase the inventory levels was a decline in sales and, of course, a subsequent decline in stock turn, which led to an even smaller inventory.

Although an organization must have a certain amount of conformity to achieve effective coordination of its parts, the existence of too many control systems overemphasizes this concept of conformity. If standards are arbitrarily set and the individual is closely controlled to conform to those standards, he will feel constrained and unhappy about his work. But if he participates in the setting of standards for his own performance, he will consider meeting those standards a challenge to his own ability.

Of course, not all standards can be set through participation. For example, it is very difficult to set a standard on the work of a punch-press operator with his participation, because this standard will then apply to other punch-press operators too. But from participation comes understanding; from understanding comes tolerance; and from tolerance comes willingness to accept. Should the manager explain to the punch-press operator how the standard was set? Some managers would answer that the punch-press operator would not understand even if it were explained to him. Others would state that the worker is not interested in knowing how standards are set. Still other managers would indicate that this involvement of the worker in setting standards will lead only to arguments and the worker's dissatisfaction.

Are these managers being realistic? The chances are that the punch-press operator is being paid some form of incentive wages, which means that the amount of money he can earn is directly controllable by this standard. The magnitude of this fact is almost overwhelming. The philosophy of an incentive wage system is that money will motivate the employee to produce more than he would on time wages. The underlying concept is that the incentive wage motivates the employee to work harder and more effectively. But if the major factor affecting whether he can or cannot attain these higher wages is not his own motivation and ability to work harder but a standard set by someone else without his understanding or acceptance, will he truly be motivated to work more effectively?

The experienced manager's position might be that the punch-press operator could not possibly be objective about a standard which is going to determine how much money he makes. This is true if the employee were given complete discretion in setting his standards. But to do that would be to abdicate the responsibility of management. The manager must still make decisions, coordinate the actions of others, and insure that conditions are such that the company will attain its objectives. The punch-press operator may be involved in the setting of the standard only to the point of understanding the methods involved. But now the standard is no longer solely an arbitrary act of management. The worker, through understanding and the degree of participation that understanding permits, will more readily accept the standard and be motivated to achieve and exceed it.

Just as democracy cannot give the individual freedom to do everything he wishes and in so doing possibly destroy society, so industry cannot permit the counterpart of democracy—participation and recognition of human dignity—to destroy organizational entity.

However, if there is nothing underhanded in the way controls are set, the manager should have no difficulty explaining their operation to his subordinates. Men fear the unknown, and all too often controls are an unknown factor which threaten their security. If this unknown factor is removed, the threat will disappear, and employees will be free to concentrate on performance.

This philosophy of control and of motivation will take many years or even decades to gain full acceptance in industry. It will require a change in attitude by countless thousands of managers. This change is not easy to accomplish, but drastic measures should not be used. Rather, change might best be initiated by a modification of the organization's philosophy about controls and the setting of standards of performance. If the entire control system changes from an overemphasis on narrow standards to a stress on accomplishment and attainment of objectives, all managers will be directly affected. As the total system of controls changes, the individual system which sets the behavior relationships between the manager and his subordinates will also change. Managers and workers alike will be motivated to pattern their behavior not merely to adhere to narrow standards but to contribute to the attainment of organizational objectives.

Controls and Decision Making

The control system is closely related to decision making or continual choice among alternatives. Controls alone cannot assure compliance with standards. Information required for effective decision making must also be available. The control system and the information network should be integrated into a master intelligence unit. Since the purpose of control is to induce patterns of behavior leading to the attainment of objectives, the control system must generate whatever information the manager requires to make the necessary decisions and to coordinate resources for attaining objectives.

A decision can only be as good as its input information. If the decision maker bases his decision on false premises and inadequate information, the decision itself obviously cannot be the correct solution to the problem.

Unfortunately, the coordination between the existing control system and the needs of the decision maker for input information is rarely effective. The control system may very well generate information to force decision making by indicating noncompliance with the plan or standards. Although the control system does provide information leading to a decision, does it give the decision maker sufficient and appropriate information to permit him to make the right decisions? The effect of the noncompliance is anxiety and possibly frustration. If the control system does not supply the requisite information, the manager may not be able to rectify the situation. This can lead to behavior that will confound the control system, rather than to action that will correct the deviations and achieve the organizational objectives.

A typical control system that utilizes a budget indicates expense variances to the manager responsible for the particular activity. Such variances are usually classified into several expense categories, but rarely does the control system go beyond that point. When the manager receives this budget variance, he is usually at a loss to know how it occurred. Obviously, the purpose of the control system is to keep him informed of such budget variances so that he can take the requisite action to correct the deviation. But where must he go to determine how the variance occurred? He may know that direct labor was higher than the budgeted figure. All too often, however, the control system does not indicate exactly where such a labor variance took place. In other words, the figure is an aggregate of all expenditures in that classification.

For example, if the manager takes it upon himself to chastise his subordinates for their failure to adhere to the standards, he may be doing them a great injustice. A number of supervisors may have carried out their responsibilities and in fact been more efficient than usual. If the manager uses criticism to gain future compliance, his subordinates will feel persecuted and will not put forth as much effort in the future. If the manager takes the route of attempting to determine exactly how and where the variance took place, he will be plagued at all turns by a lack of information. Unless he has facts with which to pursue his inquiry, he will receive only platitudes from his subordinates. In fact, they themselves may not know the reasons for unsatisfactory performance.

In this illustration, the control system, through its labor variance report, certainly indicated the manager's lack of performance, but did not necessarily elicit behavior patterns to insure attainment of objectives. The fault lies in the limited scope of the control system.

It is not enough to collect statistics indicating performance or nonperformance of a task. The control system must also provide intelligence or information to assist the manager in correcting the cause of the nonperformance. In this illustration, what was required was better coordination of the needs of the manager for information and the needs of the total organization for compliance. Both should be satisfied in the one control system.

Leadership and Control

Controls and standards of performance relate directly to the exercise of leadership and the effective motivation of subordinates. Controls can direct behavior toward the narrower performance to standards rather than toward the broader attainment of institutional objectives.

The leadership skills required to understand and utilize the control process are closely related to a basic understanding of human needs and motivation. Since controls in effect evaluate behavior by relating performance to pre-established standards, a rational process can lead to emotional consequences. But the latter can be good as well as bad. If the controls are used to punish, both those controls and the leadership responsible for them will be rejected. If the controls are designed to capture motivational factors and to satisfy human needs, both they and the leader will be accepted.

Controls themselves are only the agency used to evaluate performance. It is the standards of performance used for measurement which are responsible for any potential discontent on the part of those being evaluated. When such standards are arrived at arbitrarily, without involvement of the persons being evaluated, an automatic rejection pattern is set in motion. Proof of this point can be found in the preoccupation of unions and management in contract negotiations over work rules and performance standards.

Leadership skills in control applications are exercised in the use of a management-by-objectives approach. Management by objectives utilizes a negotiation between the boss and his subordinate. They discuss the initial set of objectives which the subordinate has developed and which he plans to achieve in the next year. Following negotiation, they agree on the objectives, which then become the standards of performance against which the control system will operate.

The manager has extensive opportunities to exercise the following leadership skills in the process of instituting management by objectives.

Perception. The leader can match his perception against that of his subordinate, since the latter has generated his personal ideas of what the job is, what priorities are involved, and his personal ambitions.

Motivation. The leader can discern the motivational pattern of the subordinate in terms of his hierarchy of needs, his development of the objectives in behavioral and rational terms, and his ability to understand the relationship of his objectives to those of the organization.

Communication. Management by objectives involves extensive two-way communication, in some instances for the first time. A skillful use of this technique can establish conditions that will lead to more effective communication in the future.

Delegation. Management by objectives is in effect an exercise in delegation, since the means to achieve the objectives must form part of the negotiated contract between superior and subordinate.

Leadership Patterns. The choice of a leadership pattern is a critical element in management by objectives. Since both the autocratic and the laissez-faire styles would result in failure of the entire program, management by objectives forces the choice of the participative style.

Behavioral Patterns in Control. The joint negotiation of the standards of performance will undoubtedly militate against the emergence of inappropriate behavior patterns. Although the failure to perform to the negotiated objectives or standards will be traumatic and unpleasant for the subordinate, his involvement in the development of the standards will result in his acceptance of the controls and the entire system.

The exercise of controls by the leader has great potential for developing behavior patterns which will be harmful to him and the organization. The application of leadership skills can guide the control system and the subsequent behavior of organizational members to the satisfaction of both institutional and personal objectives.

7

Effective communication is a major prerequisite of effective leadership. The exercise of leadership skills requires two-way communication to perceive, to motivate, to counsel. The elimination of barriers to communication—hierarchy, role expectations, prejudgment, and egocentrism—requires the conscious and deliberate application of leadership skills.

Effective Communication for Leadership

EFFECTIVE COMMUNICATION can be defined simply as the simultaneous, identical understanding of the content and intent of a message by the sender and the receiver:

Sender	Message	Receiver	Message
A →	B →	C →	B

In the diagram above, both sender A and receiver C have the same message, B. A more common occurrence is diagrammed below, where sender A sends message B, but receiver C receives message D.

Sender	Message	Receiver	Message
A →	B →	C →	D

An illustration of different messages occurred when the president of a small company implemented a profit-sharing plan. His

Effective Communication for Leadership 113

motives had little to do with using the plan as an incentive or as a way of avoiding unionization. Rather, he honestly wished to share his good fortune with his employees.

He called a special meeting of his seventy-five employees, the majority of whom were both unskilled and members of minority groups. He stated, "Men, I have wonderful news for you. I have been able to develop a profit-sharing plan so that every man in this room will receive a fair proportion of the company profits. For example, if our profits remain the same as in the past few years, any one of you who remains in the company thirty years will have $200,000 in his own profit-sharing fund when he retires." After some further enthusiastic remarks, the president adjourned the meeting.

Later, the following conversation took place between two employees about the president's announcement:

EMPLOYEE ONE: Man, what a fantastic company. The president sure is a generous fellow when you figure he owns the whole company.

EMPLOYEE TWO: Sure, it's a lousy company. They got so much money they give it away.

How could such a clear message, and one that seemed so favorable to the receiver, become so garbled?

It is interesting to note that communication and leadership have similar definitions:

Leader	Objective	Follower	Action toward Objective
A →	B →	C →	B

Leadership has been effectuated when leader A with objective B is able to persuade follower C to take action B toward that objective. Obviously, the *persuasion* requires communication. The implementation of leadership skills requires the subordinate's cooperation and involvement, which in turn requires communication between leader and subordinate. If communication is ineffective, leadership will also be ineffective.

Many companies use AVOs (Avoid Verbal Orders) to stress the importance of using written rather than oral communication in order to prevent problems. The following case illustrates the substitution of written for oral communication.

Interoffice Memorandum

TO: All Foremen and Supervisors   COPIES: All Manufacturing Managers
FROM: Vice-President, Manufacturing

Due to the excessive use of overtime in the last quarter, all overtime requests are to be countersigned by me personally.

A. Smith
Vice-President, Manufacturing

After they received this memo, three foremen were heard discussing overtime requests:

FIRST FOREMAN: I understand that all hell broke loose between old man Smith and the president. Apparently Smith was told to lower his costs or it was curtains for him.

SECOND FOREMAN: You guys got it all wrong. The whole system's been changed with the new boys in the controller's office demanding authorizations before putting in a profit center approach.

THIRD FOREMAN: Whatever the reason, I'll tell you one thing. I'm not putting in for overtime, since I figure Smitty will jump down my throat. Instead, I'm going to politic to add a couple of new guys to my group to make sure I meet schedule.

Did the written memo avoid communication problems? Certainly all the foremen understood the part of the message that called for their overt action in authorizing overtime. The problem was that their actions were influenced by their *interpretation* of the written communication. But it is unlikely that the actions which the vice-president of manufacturing intended will be those taken by the foremen. The vice-president undoubtedly wanted to cut costs, but the actions of the third foreman will lead to higher rather than lower costs.

Communication Filters

Unfortunately, communication is not the simple speaking and hearing of words and sentences. Each man creates for himself a set of filters which greatly affect the transmission of communication from one individual to another. Figure 7-1 diagrams this relationship, which consists of a double filtering effect. The sender's filter causes him to project ideas and concepts which are related to his personal frame of reference rather than to that of the receiver. For example, the sender may tend to oversimplify problems and relationships which may actually be complex, difficult, and even threatening to others. His communication patterns, choice of words, and general attitude all convey this oversimplification.

The sender in this illustration does not recognize the point of view or frame of reference of the receiver and will undoubtedly convey the wrong message. But the receiver too has barriers to communication; his filters make him tend to overcomplicate the issues so that he fails to receive the message. The result of these filter sets

Figure 7-1
Individual Filters and the Communication Process

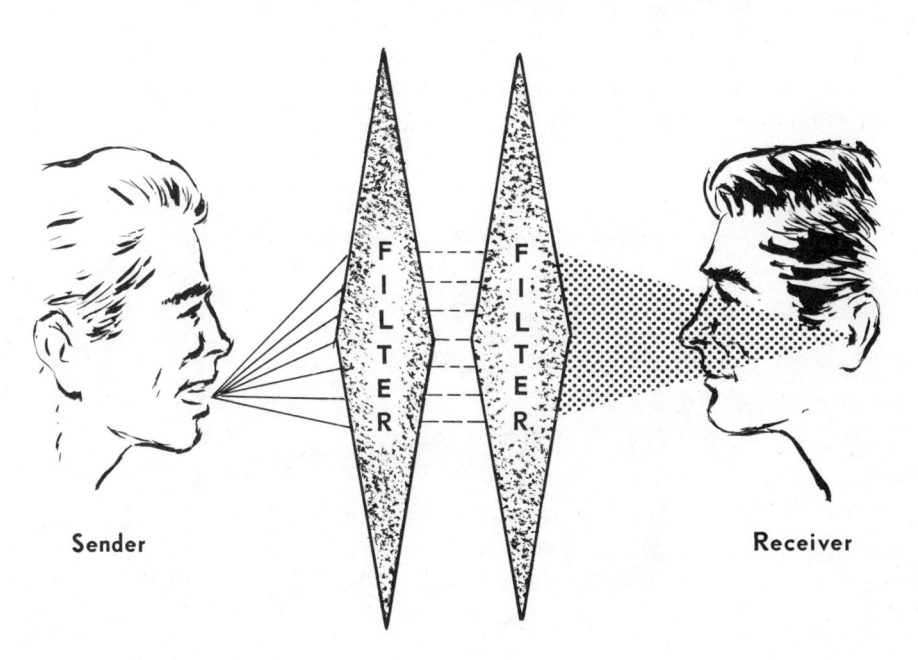

is not only the failure in communication but also, and far more important, the failure of the sender to generate appropriate action by the receiver.

Each man's frame of reference colors and conditions his reaction to events affecting him and greatly influences his actions and decisions. A frame of reference is the amalgam of the influence of his parents and family background, his educational experiences, his present and previous work conditions, and the general cultural influences of his particular city and country. This amalgam generates attitudes, to which are added but a small proportion of generally accepted facts, as illustrated in Figure 7-2.

Although even so-called facts are subject to interpretation and individual perception, usually agreement can be reached on some basic facts in a business firm. Each situation and individual will have a different relationship to the facts and attitudes, which are given as one set in Figure 7-2. Unfortunately, an additional critical point is that a comparison of the frames of reference of many senders and receivers would indicate disagreement about the particular set of facts used by each.

Barriers to Communication

One of the greatest barriers to communication is the egocentric tendency of all human beings to view every activity from a highly

Figure 7-2
The Individual's Frame of Reference: Facts and Attitudes

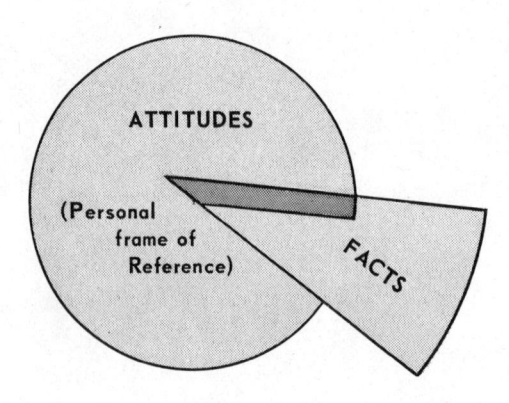

It could be argued that the company was at fault in hiring both temporary and permanent help, that the personnel director was insensitive to human needs and motivation, and that Mary just did not listen carefully in the initial interview. All these points may be true, but they do not alter the fact that the communication was rejected because it was a threat to the recipient.

Past bad experiences in communication can lead to rejection of subsequent messages and to development of barriers against them. For example, an overly enthusiastic boss might make a series of promises to his employees which he does not honor. This condition will lead the employees to distrust any future communication of the same type from the boss. This is one of the most difficult of all communication barriers to overcome. Perhaps it is too reminiscent of the boy who cried wolf once too often.

Zones of Communication

Generally, the barriers to communication are critical only in what can be termed the barrier zone, as depicted in Figure 7-4. The free zone allows direct communication without barriers, both because of the leader's skill in communicating and because the message itself does not significantly affect the receiver. The problem for the leader is to determine which category is applicable for the particular communication he wishes to make.

The free zone usually applies to the routine communications of day-to-day operations. Fortunately, in the established long-term relationships in most close-knit smaller sections of the organization, the communication channels have become so well accepted that an easy flow of communication exists without too many misinterpretations. However, this very ease often blinds the leader to subtle changes in the flow and understanding of messages.

This failure to recognize the changes in communication happened to a manager who originally had one highly competent and trusted subordinate. When the latter became overburdened with work, the manager decided that a second submanager should be hired. The first submanager was directly involved in the selection process and agreed openly and wholeheartedly with the manager's choice of the new man and the organizational change.

Figure 7-4
Barrier and Free Zones in Communication

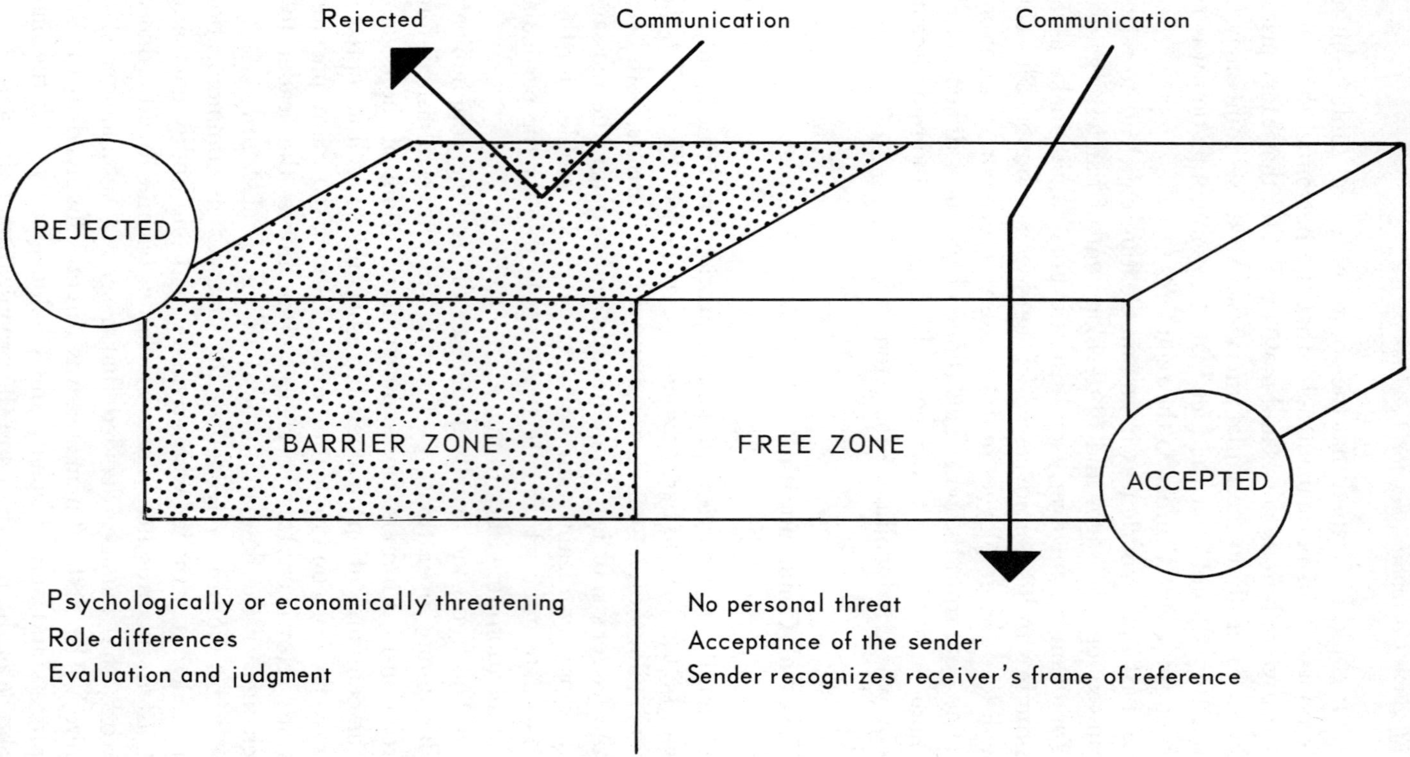

Communication — Accepted ———→ ACCEPTED

FREE ZONE

- No personal threat
- Acceptance of the sender
- Sender recognizes receiver's frame of reference

Communication — Rejected ———→ REJECTED

BARRIER ZONE

- Psychologically or economically threatening
- Role differences
- Evaluation and judgment

Six months later, the trusted subordinate wrote a formal letter of resignation to the manager. The latter was dumbfounded not only by the resignation but also by the manner in which it was tendered. He spent considerable time reflecting on his relationship with his subordinate, which had seemed to remain as good as it was before the extra man was hired. But further contemplation caused the manager to recognize a significant fact. Before the addition of the new man, the manager had always been available to his subordinate; after the new man joined the staff, the manager had to divide his time between the two submanagers. He recollected that at the beginning of his relationship with his longer-term subordinate, they had often had misunderstandings and miscommunication, but that they had solved these problems in rather emotional, lengthy conferences. The manager concluded that he had taken his long-term subordinate for granted and assumed free-zone communications that no longer existed.

This case illustrates that the leader must constantly re-examine and re-evaluate the effectiveness of his communications.

Symbolism and Language

Even the most careful use of a dictionary cannot eliminate misunderstanding and miscommunication. Words and the concepts and ideas that words connote have different meanings to different people. To understand this phenomenon, consider the actions of the anti-defamation leagues of various ethnic groups in areas such as advertising.

Words are used to represent ideas, and because a number of words are used to embellish any conversation or written message, mixed signals and misinterpretation can result. Let the reader conjure up a picture of the document described in the following sentences:

1. The document was thick, detailed, and heavily documented.
2. The interesting document was thick, detailed, and heavily documented.
3. The document was thick, detailed, and poorly written.

The first statement is essentially neutral, but implies that the document is boring reading. The second statement, by adding the word "interesting," changes the meaning to offer some possible excitement in reading a carefully researched paper. The third statement would make a reader tend to reject the document. Language, then, provides both specific, descriptive meanings and connotations for evaluation.

It is also difficult to use language with precision because the dictionary meaning of a word does not necessarily clarify the real meaning in the context in which it is used. East European countries use the term "democracy" (democratic republic) in quite a different way from West European countries. Resorting to a dictionary will fail to clarify the term "democracy": "1. Government by the people: a form of government in which the supreme power is vested in the people and exercised by them or by their elected agents under a free electoral system. 2. A state having such a form of government. 3. A state in which the supreme power is vested in the people and exercised directly by them rather than by elected representatives. 4. A state of society characterized by formal equality of rights and privileges. 5. Political or social equality; democratic spirit. 6. The common people of a community as distinguished from any priviliged class; the common people with respect to their political power." [1]

It would be difficult for the West European to carry on an intelligent conversation with his East European counterpart about democracy, even if they used the same dictionary.

In the business firm, the variety of different meanings or interpretations of words may lead to a lack of real communication. The term "participative" may mean "advisory" to one manager and "shared authority" to another. What can the manager do about this potential misunderstanding of vocabulary? The first rule is that he must not take the meanings of certain key words or concepts for granted. The second rule is that he must listen for the reaction of the receiver. The third rule is that he must test the actual receipt of the communication by some playback, such as, "Let's summarize what we have agreed to in this meeting."

To illustrate the first rule, let us return to the written memo on overtime which was sent out by the vice-president of manufactur-

[1] *The Random House Dictionary of the English Language* (New York: Random House, Inc., 1967).

ing. What was his original intent in issuing that memo? The answer was really given in the memo itself, but was apparently misunderstood by its recipients. The accent was on the word "excessive," so apparently the vice-president did not intend to forbid *all* overtime. But he broke the first rule when he took for granted the meaning of such a commonly understood concept as overtime. How could he have prevented this misunderstanding? One answer is that he might have been more precise in his language. But was he not precise and even succinct? Another answer would be that he should have been more explicit. He might have documented his memo with specific examples of the types of overtime which he considered excessive, but this would entail the risk of not providing a sufficiently exhaustive list. Furthermore, he would be introducing a different method of management, in which the decision-making authority for certain actions is removed from the foreman. It could also be argued that the original memo did this by demanding a countersignature.

The result of this analysis is that the memo fails to provide any two-way communication; therefore, the sender is unsure of the real impact of his message. A man who has reached the vice-presidential level should realize the potential ineffectiveness of this form of communication and the distorted actions that might result. He should realize the necessity of sharing a great deal more information with the foremen and other managers and the need for some form of two-way communication to evoke the action which would be best for the total organization.

This leads to the second rule—the need to listen for or to ascertain the reaction of the recipient. The vice-president could have used one of two methods to monitor the reaction. The first, a two-way discussion with his principal subordinates so that they, in turn, could communicate to their subordinates, is by far a more economical use of the vice-president's time, but could lead to a filtering of the communication and perhaps even greater misunderstanding. However, this is the normal process of communication in the managerial hierarchy and it must be honed and refined to become effective if the organization itself is to be effective. The vice-president might still want to monitor the effectiveness of his communication by discussing the message with some of the foremen, or by feedback sessions with his subordinates.

The second means of monitoring the reaction is to hold a series of meetings with all his managerial groups on a cross-section basis that would include a number of levels of the managerial hierarchy. These meetings would perhaps pose the problem of overtime and the vice-president's solution, and then would elicit the reactions of the group to that solution. Here the vice-president still runs the danger of miscommunication, since the status and hierarchial barriers to communication still exist. Furthermore, the result could be a total misinterpretation if such meetings were not normal practice in the firm. In other words, the fact that a meeting was necessary might confirm the foremen's suspicions that a tremendous crisis was occurring.

This analysis indicates that the potential for misunderstanding is indeed high, almost to the point where you are damned if you do, and damned if you don't. To establish truly effective communication, a number of measures must be taken over a long period of time.

The third rule—testing the effectiveness of the communication through some playback—has been partially covered by the vice-president's monitoring of its receipt in his meetings with his subordinates either collectively or individually. Specifically, the vice-president could ask questions such as: What will be the effect of reducing overtime on the meeting of delivery dates? Will it be necessary to add new employees? Is there some way to classify overtime to minimize the amount of countersigning necessary? The vice-president could even ask his subordinates to play the communication back directly. But without some further elaboration, the same effect—inappropriate actions by the foremen—could be the result of both the conference and the short written memo.

The manager will frequently find himself in situations where the actual result of the communication is far different from what was intended. Since the manager is the one who will suffer most from ineffective communication, the onus must be on him to develop more effective communication techniques. The result of the vice-president's memo would be disastrous for him, since his efforts to solve the problem of excessive overtime will lead to a new set of problems which may be more difficult to solve.

At this point, the manager interested in developing better communication skills may think that either the frequency of miscommunication is greatly overstated in these pages, or, alternatively, that effective communication is impossible to achieve. Let there be no question that miscommunication is the more common occurrence in business, and in fact, in every aspect of life. Recent studies have shown that the manager spends some 70 percent of his time receiving communication and some 45 percent initiating it. It would be interesting to conjecture how much of this communication was ineffective.

Communication Behavior

Understanding communication behavior is critical to the development of effective communication practices. One type of behavior involved in communication is adaptive behavior, which is the behavioral pattern of people who recognize the need to conform their behavioral patterns to those acceptable to the group or the leader. In communication, adaptive behavior takes the form of both verbal and nonverbal actions by the recipient to indicate to the sender that the communication is being accepted. These actions may include social noises, such as "oh yes," "really," "that's right," "okay"; or of responses such as nodding, looking the communicator in the eye, and simulating attentiveness. The communicator is often lulled into a false sense of security by these responses, and fails to reinforce his communication to insure its receipt.

Another important aspect is the behavioral pattern of the parties involved. The proverb, It is not what you do but how you do it, could be restated to read, It is not what you say but how you say it. The attitudes of people are generally quite apparent from tone and volume of voice, posture of the body, and facial expressions. Unfortunately, we are rarely able to examine these factors in ourselves, and may very well present a different image from the one we wish to project. The world, however, deals not in reality but in the perception of reality. The manager must ascertain what image he is projecting if he wishes to transmit his intended communication.

How can the manager know what perceptions others have about his communication? One way to find out is to have a particularly open and friendly relationship with a fellow manager who can provide a reading on how the communication was received. Another method is to enroll in a sensitivity training program which helps most participants develop considerable insight and self-awareness. Finally, the manager can observe the recipients to see if they took action different from that intended.

Nonverbal communication behavior is a critical indicator for social perception. The effective communicator controls his nonverbal messages just as closely as his verbal in order to avoid misunderstanding.

Another consideration is that of role expectation or stereotyping. Certain behavioral patterns are expected of people based upon their institutional, personal, or professional roles. When the union organizer behaves like the college professor, and the college professor like the union organizer, communication will be hindered or even rejected. Role expectation is really part of society's norms; therefore, the manager must be careful not to make abrupt and serious departures from his expected role. This is particularly true in new situations where the manager may have to play the part, at least initially, or seriously endanger his potential effectiveness.

Stereotyping is not restricted to role expectations, but is often based on physical characteristics as well. The manager must carefully guard against the influence of physical stereotyping in his own receipt and interpretation of communications. When he is the initiator, he must recognize the potential tendency of the recipients to stereotype him.

A Prescription for Effective Communication

Since effective communication is a prerequisite for effective leadership, the manager should develop the following techniques:

Two-way Communication. The manager, desiring to establish some concepts or ideas with others, thinks of communication as the simple provision of information. He may choose his words carefully, and even adapt his behavior to support his communication, but he usually believes that if he understands the point, so will his listener. When the receiver attempts to establish a two-way communication link, the manager is inclined to pay little if any attention to the information offered.

The establishment of two-way communication takes a great deal of conscious effort and concentration by the manager who is used to the more common one-way, "tell them" type of communication. The first rule is to establish the conditions which will encourage two-way communication. To do this, the manager must recognize the various barriers to communication and must provide adequate, uninterrupted time for exchanges with subordinates. There should be no interruptions by the telephone or by other people. Of course, communications which are nonthreatening and repetitive, or which contain routine information, do not require such elaborate and careful treatment.

The manager must also establish a psychological environment which will encourage two-way communication. He must put the other person at ease, which often requires social and general comments at first. When the discussion becomes task oriented, the manager should use phrases like, "We have a problem," or "Our market position is deteriorating," rather than, "You have a problem." This is not manipulation, since the manager and his subordinate do share responsibility for any failure by the latter.

There is also a need to avoid either generalities which cannot be dealt with or any personal accusations which will only serve to end the attempt at two-way communication. It is best to deal with specific and factual information. The manager may tend to present his conclusions rather than the issues and relevant facts. Because it is difficult for a subordinate to refute or even discuss conclusions provided by his boss, the manager should always keep in mind the objectives of his communication, which are to persuade the subordinate to accept the message or to negotiate a communication acceptable to both the manager and the subordinate.

After the manager presents the issue and relevant facts, he should ask his subordinate to corroborate or amend them as he sees fit. This approach—the immediate establishment of common premises or facts—is critical to the effectiveness of the communication, and is usually far less emotional and threatening to either party than other techniques.

The second rule is the absolute necessity for the manager to listen. Listening requires discipline, concentration, and an ability to perceive the real meaning behind the words. After the manager develops the problems or issues and perhaps some alternative courses of action, he must stop talking. Even the most reticent of men abhor long silences, and when the manager keeps quiet, the subordinate will be forced to communicate. The manager's tendency at this point may be to return to his role of communicator and to dominate the situation. But the objective of two-way communication is to develop understanding between two people. The manager must be vitally interested in understanding his subordinate's frame of reference so that interaction can lead to effective two-way communication.

The third rule is to terminate the discussion with a summary of the points which both parties have accepted, such as the action to be taken on a decision, or the implementation phase of an objective. This summary can often be phrased with considerable precision.

Psychological Aspects of Communication. Man as an egocentric being considers every action solely in terms of how it affects him. The manager as a communicator is as guilty of this egocentrism as his subordinates, but if he is sophisticated, he sees his subordinates as an extension of his own egocentric circle. This concept is depicted in Figure 7-5, where the larger circle illustrates the broad range of interests of the manager who realizes that his success is inextricably tied up with that of his subordinates.

The employee tends to evaluate all communication on the basis of its potential impact on his job or his position. In other words, he is highly subjective. Furthermore, he tends to react more strongly to a communication which affects him deeply, and to shut off any communication which he feels has no relevance to him. This failure to listen may also occur when he thinks the information is personally threatening.

The importance of this psychological aspect of communication cannot be overemphasized. The manager must ask himself, How will this information affect my subordinate (or associate managers or boss)? Past experiences will provide insights about potential reactions and will enable the manager to predict possible reactions to the new communication.

The point of predicting the reaction is not to avoid the communication but rather to consider how best to handle its transmission. Unfortunately, some managers use this technique to avoid any confrontation and therefore do not establish the communication. Realistically, however, the manager is paid to handle tough problems and he cannot avoid communication just because it will be unpleasant or difficult. When he recognizes the potential of emotional or highly subjective reactions, he must utilize communication techniques such as: (1) raising the issue and asking the subordinate to study the problem, including alternative courses of action; (2)

Figure 7-5
The Egocentric Nature of Man

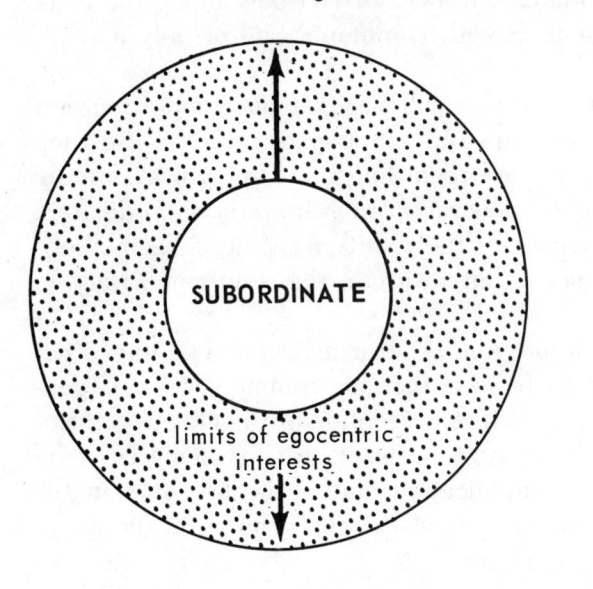

Rejection or lack of involvement with others

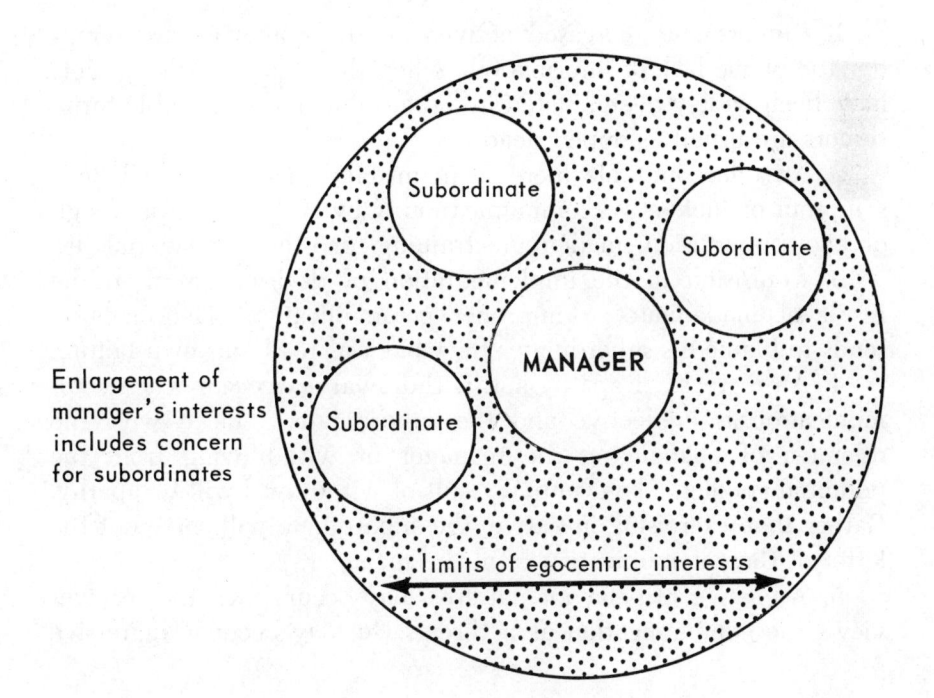

SUBORDINATE

limits of egocentric interests

Enlargement of manager's interests includes concern for subordinates

Subordinate

Subordinate

MANAGER

Subordinate

limits of egocentric interests

facing the issue directly and forcing it into the open, recognizing the potential of an emotional outburst; or (3) developing the issue slowly over a period of time with communication of only a small part at a time.

At this point, some managers will say that one should face up squarely to an unpleasant issue and call a spade a spade. But they should remember that they are regarding the communication only from their personal point of view rather than from the subordinate's. The effective manager considers the results and adjusts his methods not to fit his personal needs but to attain the results necessary in each case.

Periodic Communication Audits. The manager, like any other human being, is likely to believe that his communication is generally effective. Since an incorrect perception of the effectiveness of communication can have devastating results, it is particularly useful to develop a personal communication audit. The first step in the audit is similar to that of the medical doctor who looks for symptoms in order to make a diagnosis:

Symptoms

1. Rumors and increased activity of the grapevine are symptomatic of the lack of information. When the accurate, official facts have been widely disseminated in a digestible and intelligible form, rumors are usually stopped dead.

2. An unaccountable increase in mistakes may very well be a symptom of ineffective communication. Obviously, it is also a sign of poor supervision, inadequate training, or other managerial ills.

3. Confusion in the implementation of decisions is often the result of inadequate or improper communication. The manager tends to blame his subordinates for what was really his own failure.

4. An increase of apathy and withdrawal may occur when communication is ineffective and the subordinate is faced with the dilemma of challenging the manager or withdrawing from the potential conflict. The eventual result of withdrawal will be apathy. Rather than exercising initiative, the subordinate will carry out the letter of the communication from the manager.

5. A change in behavior patterns may occur when the receiver views the communication as a threat. He may become aggressive

or cold and hostile. This reaction is one of the most common symptoms of poor communication and has been experienced by everyone in one form or another.

6. An increase in the subordinates' demands for personal contact may be caused by poor or inadequate information. Employees may be unwilling to make decisions, preferring to refer them to a higher authority.

7. The subordinate who makes frequent demands on the manager for reassurance of his personal worth is not necessarily betraying a feeling of insecurity. His demands may be a sign of the manager's failure to communicate effectively.

8. An increase in the general anxiety level is often the result of poor, inadequate, or even incorrect communication. Since anxiety is a general rather than a specific feeling of uneasiness, it is difficult to get subordinates to articulate what is wrong.

9. A need to repeat communication at a later time is obviously a symptom of poor communication, and is readily apparent even without a communication audit.

The second step in the audit is a detailed examination of individual communication practices, which are listed here in summary form for easy reference.

Communication Practices

1. Understand the recipient's frame of reference.
2. Provide the right conditions for an exchange of communications.
3. Recognize the fact that written communication does not eliminate communication problems.
4. Avoid evaluation and judgment, and recognize this tendency in recipients.
5. Consider role, prestige, and status barriers to communication.
6. Determine the threat potential in the communication.
7. Accept the fact that language is not precise and that words have different meanings to different people.
8. Recognize that nonverbal behavior conditions the response perhaps even more than the verbal message itself.
9. Provide for feedback from and involvement in the communication process.

The increasing complexity of business has resulted in an almost excessive use of the coordinating device of conferences or committees. The generalist-manager must rely more and more on staff specialists, who in turn need cross fertilization of ideas to provide broader-gauge answers to problems. The best method for achieving this cross fertilization and interaction is the management conference.

8

Conference Leadership

THE DECISIVE ENTREPRENEUR of the nineteenth century has given way to his twentieth-century counterpart, who initially cultivated leadership skills to motivate and develop his employees as individuals, and who finally developed conference leadership skills to coordinate and integrate groups of people meeting in conference. Because an increasing percentage of top executive time is now devoted to conferences of one type or another, there is a critical need to develop conference leadership skills.

Conference Member Roles

The elements involved in conference leadership can best be developed by categorizing the typical personalities who attend conferences, both as leaders and as participants.

Conference leaders range from the highly autocratic to the overly permissive:

The Father Figure. As a conference leader, he feels he should be solicitous of everyone, asking each in turn to express an opinion. He is of the opinion that he must take care of his "boys." He really has very little interest in their opinions, but thinks it is a good idea to get them together to keep up morale. His leadership usually creates frustration and eventually apathy, and little of constructive use is achieved.

Mr. Human Relations. This conference leader has read that participative management is the vogue, and he is determined to keep up with the times. He considers the meeting a chore to be dispensed with as quickly as possible. All except neophyte members soon realize that the conference he leads is just an exercise which provides sufficient input to satisfy his ego needs.

The Manipulator. This man has already made up his mind about the issues, and uses the conference to manipulate others to support his point of view. He permits maximum participation by everyone, but never resolves differences of opinion except when he can bend them to support his original conclusions. He uses the conference as a sledge hammer to convince his superiors of the involvement and support of all his people. The conferees realize they are being manipulated, but are powerless to take overt counteraction. Their apathy spills over into the day-to-day actions of the group, with a resulting demoralizing effect.

The Autocrat. This conference leader stifles any meaningful discussion by judging or evaluating every comment or suggestion made by the conferees. As a result, no one is willing to make any truly innovative contributions. He is also totally defensive of his position, believing that most remarks are challenges to his authority.

The Popularity Seeker. This man is unwilling to exercise leadership if there is any challenge from the group. In his attempt to placate everyone, he is caught in the cross fire between two opposing groups. The result is either a bitter and unrestrained battle between opposing groups or an unwritten agreement to avoid controversial subjects.

The Permissive Leader. The term "leader" is a misnomer here, since there is no leadership, only anarchy and chaos. Because of this man's lack of leadership, the group does not search for consensus or conclusions, and achieves nothing in terms of constructive solutions to issues. The conferees are usually frustrated but not necessarily apathetic, since each has an opportunity to say what he pleases.

Conference members range from the cooperative and helpful to the highly obstructive:

The Incessant Talker. This conferee attempts to dominate the discussion and rarely if ever listens to the other participants. If the conference leader does not act to stop the incessant talker, the other conferees will become bored and fail to take part in the conference.

The One-opinion Conferee. This man has only one opinion and will not budge from it, no matter what counterarguments are presented. He is extremely difficult to handle in the conference, and must be dealt with on an individual basis outside the meeting.

The Frustrated Leader. This conferee constantly challenges the conference leader and attempts to usurp his role for personal ego reasons rather than for constructive purposes. The leader can handle this man best by direct action during the conference.

The Hidden Agenda Conferee. This man wishes to subvert the purpose of the conference to his own ends. He has a predetermined plan of action or at least a conviction to which he wishes to bend the other conferees. He will antagonize them, and must be dealt with firmly by the conference leader.

The Brownie-point Conferee. This man watches the conference leader and any other powerful figures to determine how he can support their positions and gain personal credits. He contributes little or nothing to the conference, is resented by the other conferees, and is often despised by those he is attempting to impress.

The Obstructionist. This man resents the time he must spend in conferences, which he considers a total waste of time. His cynicism often leads to a negative attitude and a generally obstructive method of discussing the issues. He is difficult to handle and may eventually contaminate the other conferees, with a resulting failure of the conference. The leader must deal directly with this man outside the conference and take whatever measures are necessary to change his behavior patterns in the conference.

Conference Leadership

The Purposes of Conferences

Obviously the decision to hold a conference or a meeting must be based on the need to achieve some purpose or objective. Would such purposes be the same for all meetings? The answer, of course, is no. Yet management usually fails to distinguish between types of meetings or conferences, and as a result many potentially useful and effective meetings become failures.

A typical and common type of meeting is the weekly staff conference, where a manager meets with all his subordinate managers to review past problems and plan for the week ahead. This meeting provides an ideal opportunity for multilateral exchanges and communication between people in horizontal, usually peer relationships rather than in vertical or hierarchial relationships. But the success of the meeting is entirely dependent on the conference leader's abilities to organize and direct the meeting.

It is critical for the conference leader to recognize the climate he must create to permit openness and a true exchange of opinions. Let us consider how such a meeting might be conducted:

CONFERENCE LEADER: As you all know, we have had some real reverses this past week and are both over budget and behind schedule. I want to get to the bottom of it. Bill, plating is one of our bottlenecks. What are you doing about it?

BILL: Chief, we had a quality problem in one of our main coatings, but we've got that licked now.

CONFERENCE LEADER: Okay, let's keep on top of it. Now, Jim, you have had excessive absenteeism and resulting overtime. What do you plan to do to solve the problem?

JIM: The Asian flu has just about peaked, so the problem should take care of itself within a week or two.

What was the climate created by this conference leader? Certainly it resulted in a one-to-one communication pattern rather than in a multilateral exchange. What was the purpose of this conference? Originally there might have been some idea that the solution to the problems might require input and action by a number of the attending managers. Or there might have been some thought that the conference would serve to keep everyone informed of the problems and solutions which might affect him.

But the leader used this conference as a monitoring device. He defined the problems and requested specific information on them or solutions to them. The result was an inquisition which was potentially threatening to the participants and possibly damaged their status among their comanagers. If the leader wanted specific information from a specific man, why did he not seek it in a two-man meeting? The only possible advantage of the larger conference was the briefing of all the submanagers on the status of problems—but this advantage must be measured in terms of the need for briefing and what useful action would result. Certainly, in the climate created in this conference, the participants would volunteer little information.

Let us examine a similar type of meeting with a different style of conference leadership:

CONFERENCE LEADER: Last week we discussed our situation, which we predicted would put us behind schedule and over budget this week. Each of us was requested to analyze his department to identify the problem areas and provide some solutions for discussion and possible implementation. Let's start with you, Bill.

BILL: In the plating department we have had a real problem in quality of some of our plating materials. I discussed this with Tom in purchasing, and he recommended a change in our specs. But this may create a problem with our customers.

CONFERENCE LEADER: John, what do you think the sales department can do to help Bill out in this coating problem?

JOHN: It won't make any difference to most of our customers, but Johnson Brothers have a special application which could cause us some trouble. I'll check them out first thing in the morning and then talk with Bill and Tom on what we can do.

In this conference the leader has adopted a sharing or participative style. He is the catalyst who organizes his conferees to discuss problems openly and to seek joint solutions. In one sense, the conference leader is still using the directive approach by focusing on the issues he feels are critical and by allocating responsibility. The conference served a number of purposes: (1) it was a communication device to keep all managers briefed on current problems and issues; (2) it was a joint problem-solving device to involve the appropriate managers in the solution of problems; (3) it was a monitoring device to keep the conference leader informed of the problem areas; and (4) it was a listening post to determine feelings and attitudes, as well as to uncover any serious friction and stress that might exist among the conferees.

Let us replay the conference with John, the sales manager, giving a different reply to the conference leader's query about the coating problem.

JOHN: Frankly, our customers won't put up with these constant changes. If we go this route, we stand to lose a number of important customers.

The conference leader has been given an important communication, but he has to interpret it to determine what action he should take. One interpretation is that there is either personal or institutional conflict between the sales and production departments. Why didn't the plating manager check with sales before the meeting, and why is sales adamant that the plating change is unacceptable to customers? There may be a long history of animosity between the two departments which the skillful conference leader could eliminate or minimize. If there is personal conflict, he has now identified it and will be able to handle it outside the meeting.

The other message is technical in nature, and informs the leader that the solution will not work and that a further search must be instituted for a viable solution.

There are other purposes of conferences and meetings: information dissemination, solicitation of ideas, persuasion of a group, group decision making, indoctrination, training and development, mutual exchange of ideas and viewpoints, and preliminary testing of ideas or plans.

This list is representative but not exhaustive. To give the manager more specific and useful guides to conference leadership, four categories of conferences are described:

The Informational Conference. The pure form of this conference has the one objective of disseminating information. Why should a conference be held to disseminate information which could be conveyed in written form? A conference is expensive, since each conferee must be paid his salary to attend. A three-hour conference for thirty higher middle-management executives would cost at least a thousand dollars.

It is obvious that the informational conference must be used only to disseminate information when such a technique is greatly superior to other information-disseminating devices. But to be effective, it must be highly organized and logistically sound. The conference leader must use every possible communicating support device, from flip charts to video tape, to convey his message dramatically and effectively.

Although the primary objective is to disseminate information, essentially unilaterally, the informational conference provides the personal contact to assure the conference leader that his message has been received. It can involve two-way communication and even discussion groups, which are normally the vehicles for the problem-solving conference. These trappings may lead to misconceptions on the part of the conferees that the informational conference offers participation in the decision-making or decision-influencing process. These misconceptions lead to frustration, and eventually to aggression or apathy.

The informational conference has been equated to authoritarian or autocratic leadership, but this view maligns a useful communication device. The critical point is that the conferees recognize the purpose of the conference and adjust their behavior accordingly. The leader, who should be dynamic and authoritative, has a major responsibility to set forth the conference objectives at the outset to allay fears of coercion and manipulation.

The informational conference should be kept short and should present only a few relatively uncomplicated concepts. It should move briskly, with reinforcement devices such as visual aids and repetition of the major issues or points. If the information requires overt action by the conferees, smaller discussion groups should be utilized to develop plans of action, and those groups should later report to the entire conference. This enables the conference leader to provide input to the small groups and to receive feedback on the actions recommended for implementation.

The Problem-solving Conference. The problem-solving conference differs from the informational conference in both content and process. Unlike the informational conference, which presents both problems and solutions with the accent on disseminating information about solutions, the problem-solving conference presents only problems or issues, and elicits the solutions from the conferees.

The leader of this type of conference is a facilitator or moderator; he plays a questioning and supporting role to elicit group solutions. He accepts and believes in the group dynamics of the conference, and practices a high degree of perceptive and social sensitivity in dealing with the participants. Although he may also serve as a resource person providing ideas, he must never dogmatically support his ideas over those of the group, or evaluate and judge the contributions of the conferees.

Most managers find it extremely difficult to change from a decisive role to that of facilitating problem solving by others. In some instances, even though the manager has changed his role, his subordinates and even his peers will not believe him in his new role, with the resulting failure of the problem-solving conference. It may take considerable time for the manager to persuade others of the seriousness of his posture as a leader of the problem-solving conference.

Under what circumstances would the problem-solving conference be effective, and what advantages would accrue to its use? As a manager becomes more experienced, he develops some ability to recognize his own strengths and weaknesses. But such self-perception needs constant updating if the manager is to avoid making costly errors. The problem-solving conference allows the manager such a check on his self-perception, since it provides him with a cross section of perceptions from many points of view about a common problem.

Another advantage of the problem-solving conference is the opportunity to pretest solutions by means of the collective judgment of the conferees. If the solutions have flaws in functional implementation, such as sales or production, they can be discarded without the cost of further checking. But this advantage can also be a disadvantage, since the group process may result in the rejection of unique, innovative solutions.

An important consideration in problem-solving conferences is the psychic income or psychological payoff from the participation and involvement of the conferees. A dependent and passive subordinate makes little personal contribution except as an extension of his manager. He is unwilling to make original contributions if the system punishes such creativity. This in turn reinforces his pattern of dependent behavior.

The skillful leader can use the problem-solving conference to instill a new independence in such passive subordinates. There will be a reinforcement of ego and self-worth, with resulting patterns of independent behavior and a willingness to exercise judgment and originality. The psychological payoff can even result in a new and more open relationship between manager and subordinate. But this new state of mind is tenuous, because each man looks suspiciously at every action of the manager to determine whether he is only putting up a facade and actually manipulating the group. The first time the manager uses problem-solving conference techniques, he must be conscious of his behavior to avoid any misperceptions by his subordinates.

The Group Decision-making Conference. Unlike the problem-solving conference, in which the manager is responsible for the final decision, the group decision-making conference places responsibility on the group for the decision. For example, a salary review committee may be responsible for arriving at group decisions on salary increases. The administrative process may make these decisions subject to the veto of the president, but that does not change the group decision-making responsibility of the committee.

Thus, the group decision-making conference places the conference leader in a peer position with the conferees. His greatest difficulty arises in sorting out hierarchical relationships and roles to permit uninhibited discussion. This problem is well illustrated by the board of directors which consists of inside directors who occupy managerial positions. Acting in concert, the board can fire the president, but when it is not in session, the president can fire members of the board who hold managerial positions in the company. It is difficult to see how the inside director can truly engage in group decision making as a member of the board of directors.

When the conference leader's hierarchical position places him in command of the majority of the conferees, his managerial role may inhibit the true group decision-making process. On the other hand, if his hierarchical role is inferior to that of many of the conferees, the higher-ranking participants may not let him act as a true conference leader.

Even when a real peer relationship exists, the dynamics of individual personality, status, and influence may thwart the group decision-making process. These factors point to great difficulty for effective conference leadership as well as for the group decision-making process. Despite such difficulties, situations exist in boards of directors, pension trust funds, and the like where group decision making is required.

The skills of the conference leader are particularly applicable in this situation, where he must play one influential person against another and create a climate in which conferees with lesser status can contribute. One such device is to elicit comment on a person-by-person basis around the conference table. The leader must also rely heavily on rules of order with a prearranged consensus-determining device such as voting. He must be very much the parliamentarian to ensure an orderly process and the clarification of facts and process.

The Mixed-objective Conference. The majority of business conferences contain elements of the informational, problem-solving, and group decision-making conferences. At what point does the conference leader change his style, and how will the conferees react to an abrupt change of leadership style? There are constraints in operation at every level of an organization which are not subject to debate or decision by the conferees. In a group decision-making conference on salaries, there are pre-established constraints on salary levels and overall amounts. In a problem-solving conference, there are limits to the solutions which can be determined by the group. What happens to the process when the conference leader informs the group about these limitations? Alternatively, what happens if the conference leader withholds such information to avoid inhibiting the conferees?

The mixed-objective conference places particularly heavy demands on the skills of the conference leader. He is dealing on a highly sensitive plane with the feelings and emotions of others. If he acts inappropriately by confusing his various conference leadership roles, he runs the risk of alienating his subordinates and fellow managers. Therefore, it is imperative that he determine what type of conference he is really holding and what effect his behavior will have on the participants and the success of the conference.

The effective leader of the mixed-objective conference must possess a high degree of sensitivity to the reactions of others so that he can determine the most appropriate course of action. Furthermore, he must think and act quickly if he is to achieve the objectives of the conference without either arousing the enmity of some conferees or expending a great deal of time to bring the conference back on course.

Planning the Conference

Although some leadership skills are common to all types of conferences, the actual behavior of the conference leader must vary, depending on the type of conference. He is hierarchically the individual designated to run the conference and be responsible for both its process and its results. The conferees expect the conference leader to provide the following:

Adequate Physical Facilities. This may sound trite, but a conference held in a hotel whose conference facilities are also contracted out for a wedding has little chance of success. The check on facilities must include factors such as the seating arrangement to permit effective interchange; the adequacy and noise level of the air conditioning; the opportunity to use multimedia visual aids effectively; the ready availability of rest rooms; and even the provision of sufficient ashtrays.

Agenda and Adequate Notice of Meeting Time and Place. What is the purpose of the meeting and what is going to be discussed? The conference leader must assure the conferees in advance that the meeting is well planned and well organized. If the conference is to be other than informational, some device is needed to permit agenda input from the conferees. The agenda must not be too extensive, and should provide supporting documents if any of the subjects to be discussed requires prior study.

Orderly and Fair Leadership. The conferee is ambivalent; he demands a great deal of personal freedom of action during the conference, and yet desires structure to develop concrete plans or solutions to problems. If the leader provides too much individual freedom of action, the result will be a chaotic meeting, with little or no resolution of issues; if he provides too much structure, discussion will be stifled and the result will be a lack of any real consensus or agreement.

Followup on Conference Recommendations. Although the conference itself may be highly successful, the lack of followup to implement recommendations or to take action will destroy its effectiveness. This fault is particularly common to government and universities, where conference recommendations often end up in the labyrinth of the administrative bureaucracy, never to see the light of day again.

Short, Well-run Conferences. There is an old saying that the mind can absorb only what the bottom can endure. Conferences must be long enough to permit adequate opportunity for discussion and the resolution of differences, but not so long as to fatigue the conferees. Obviously, such time limits restrict the number of conferees in the problem-solving or decision-making conference to twelve or fifteen.

Developing Conference Leadership Skills

When leadership moves from a one-to-one interface to a multiple interaction, a number of subtle but important differences take place. The relationship of superior to subordinate is relatively well defined, and even one-to-one peer relationships have a great deal of certainty.

When the manager discusses issues with his subordinate, the dimension of the problem, the relative decision-making powers, and even the personality attributes of each man are all fairly certain. As the number of persons involved increases, the permutations and combinations of interrelationships move the situation toward uncertainty along a continuum.

When the leader is faced with a conference situation, he must use an appropriate leadership style, requiring a differing set of skills. Since it is difficult to adjust to uncertainty, the manager may find this situation disquieting, and may revert to his normal but perhaps inappropriate leadership style. A major expectation of subordinates is that the manager will continue in his role of making evaluation and final judgment. This is true whether the manager delegates or uses participative and consultative techniques of leadership. But evaluative leadership, when carried over into a problem-solving conference, will not create the appropriate climate for success. Rather, the manager as conference leader must dispel any fears of evaluation and must minimize his judgmental position to encourage involvement by the conferees.

The best way to illustrate conference leadership skills is to simulate an actual conference from its inception.

Step 1: Definition of the Problem. Even standing committees must start with a definition of the problem if they are to come into existence in a logical and rational way. This definition usually requires some research and investigation to determine the problem's magnitude, its direction, and some range of possible solutions. Often such research and investigation should be undertaken by a staff agency which has the time and possibly the budget to do this work.

Management has a tendency to appoint a committee or develop a conference in order to define the problem. This approach creates conditions of great uncertainty not only for the conference leader but also for the conferees. Furthermore, it is extremely expensive, since the conferees will not have established facts which have been analyzed and will make unfounded statements about problems. A case in point was the meeting a president held with his principal subordinates to determine why sales and profits had fallen drastically in the past three months. The meeting consisted of a series of highly disputed opinions based on few or no facts. The president terminated the session with the observation that it was obvious that no one knew why profits and sales had declined, and he chastised all present for their failure to provide the appropriate answers. But it was the president who should have been censured. He had failed to define the problem adequately and to provide preconference materials and assignments that would have created the conditions to make the conference a success.

Step 2: Is a Conference the Appropriate Vehicle to Solve the Problem? Conferences and committees are expensive, difficult to control, and relatively ineffective in task formulation and achievement. On the other hand, they can be excellent motivators and communication disseminators, and can be effective in preventing potential pitfalls and in producing a range of solutions to problems. Why appoint a committee to do a job? One reason is to provide representative input from those involved; for example, a problem might have financial, marketing, and production aspects which should be discussed. Another reason is to allay the fears of various branches or parts of the organization that action will be taken which would be detrimental to any one group.

But reasons like these have proliferated the appointments of innumerable committees which offer limited return on a major investment of time and money. The conference or committee should be used sparingly, and only when it is the optimal vehicle for solving the problem. Basically, this means that the group process must be far superior to the individual process. There must be reasons established why the individual assignment cannot elicit the information required for the solution of the problem.

Effective utilization of committees and conferences requires the operation of the synergistic effect of 2 plus 2 equals 5, which is usually applied to mergers and acquisitions. Will the sum of the effort of the conferees greatly exceed the product of its individual members? This is a difficult question to answer, but it is critical to the effective use of conferences.

Step 3: Choosing the Membership of the Conference. The informational conference will not have the same problems of choice as the problem-solving or decision-making conference. When in doubt in the informational conference, it is best to include those whose return is marginal, only considering the potential return for the time investment. Because most informational conferences will give some status benefit to conferees, their inclusion may have a motivating effect.

In contrast, the membership of the problem-solving or decision-making conference is critical to its success. Members must be chosen on the basis of the contribution they can make to the resolution of the problems or issues. Obviously, this supports Step 1, since membership could not be determined on the basis of individual contribution without a well-thought-out definition of the problem. Contribution has a number of dimensions, including the possession of appropriate knowledge, an ability to communicate ideas, analytical and synthesizing skills, and a positive attitude toward the group process. Few men possess all these attributes, but an attempt should be made to choose the conferees from among those possessing them to a greater degree than others in the organization.

Step 4: Planning the Conference. The conference leader must set the stage for an effective conference by extensive planning and preparation. The demands placed on him during the actual meeting make it difficult to remedy any planning failures in the heat of discussion.

His planning must include some projection of the number of meetings to be held, the amount of time required, the possible use of briefing techniques to start the conference, the possibility of making individual assignments in advance of the meeting, and whether subcommittees might be utilized as a device to generate position papers for the next meeting.

Step 5: Running the Conference. The actual leadership of the conference is the crucial test. It is critical to establish at the outset how long the conference will last, whether refreshments are to be served, and most important, how the conference is to be run. After preliminary explanations of the ground rules, the conference leader should introduce the purpose of the conference. This action will reinforce the importance of a businesslike approach to the conference and confirm his role as conference leader.

He should next refer to the agenda and start discussion on the first item, perhaps with a question directed at a particular conferee on whom he can depend for a comprehensive statement. The tendency in the conference will be to depart from the agenda in tangential directions. The conference leader must always bring the group back to the issue under discussion, but must guard against alienating the conferees by high-handed methods. An excerpt from a conference will illustrate this problem.

The conference leader has introduced a problem of consumer acceptance of new product A. The issue is how to interpret the evidence over the past three months on a test market introduction:

MARKET RESEARCH MANAGER: The evidence is quite clear that A is appealing primarily to the middle to lower income group.

PRODUCT DEVELOPMENT MANAGER: It was our original plan to straddle the average income group, and we designed the product with that in mind.

SALES MANAGER: We told you that the price was too high and that we had to lower our costs if we were going to break into that market.

The conference leader sees that the discussion is beginning to drift away from the central issue, and decides to direct it back:

CONFERENCE LEADER: But price is not our central issue, and if we continue in this direction we will not answer the real problem of consumer acceptance.

SALES MANAGER: What do you mean, price is not our central issue? If we had priced the product correctly in the first place, we wouldn't even have to waste time on this meeting.

Obviously, the conference leader's remark was rejected and even resented, and the conference got even more out of hand. Let us assume the conference leader decided to wait longer to assert leadership because he thought the situation was not yet deteriorating. The next remark after the sales manager's comment on the need to lower costs was picked up by the production manager:

PRODUCTION MANAGER: Our costs were never an issue. We built the product exactly as specified within the time and cost limits given to us. Isn't that right, Product Development?

PRODUCT DEVELOPMENT MANAGER: Sure, I know you sales people wanted a lower price, but market research gave us the price range where our competition was most vulnerable. I grant you that we could have come in at a lower price, but other than upgrading some slightly lower income people to buy A, we really hit our target.

The conference leader has allowed the participants to re-establish the direction of the conference. It is better to err on the side of too little direction than on too much in conference leadership. But let us suppose that the sales manager came back strongly on the price-cost issue and was supported by the cost control manager, to the point where the logical and sensible argument of the product development manager was submerged and unable to influence the direction of the conference back on course.

The conference leader sees that positions are being both polarized and solidified. He must now reassert his leadership, but how? In the original example of such assertion, the leader himself directly challenged an erring member and found his own leadership challenged in turn. This is an important lesson: The conference leader rarely should establish a position as his own; instead, he should support an existing position by calling a halt to the discussion and determining the progress being made toward solutions. In this illustration, the conference leader wishes to terminate the price discussion and focus on the actual results of the test market introduction:

CONFERENCE LEADER: I wonder if it might be in order to stop our discussion and see where we are on the first item of our agenda. As you remember, our task was to interpret the information received to date on our test market introduction of product A. Apparently we have missed our target slightly by upgrading the lower income groups rather than appealing primarily to middle income groups. This has led us to question whether the pricing was right in the first instance, but apparently we cannot really look at the price issue if what market research tells us is true about our competitors' products. Perhaps the question now is, what effect will this slightly changed market segment have on the long-range acceptance of A and on our products in the marketplace? Maybe sales could give us some insight on this issue?

The conference leader has: (1) re-emphasized the structure of the conference by referring to the agenda and the issue; (2) summarized both sides of the disagreement, emphasizing the more appropriate position; and (3) disarmed his potential major adversary by deferring to his judgment on an important part of the issue. It is possible, but unlikely, that the sales manager will reject this play. Even if he does, there is every chance that the weight of the conferees will be thrown on the conference leader's side as a reasonable position.

Some critics of these techniques might charge that the conference leader is aborting the real purpose of the discussion, and manipulating the conference to his own ends. This accusation may be true, but even those with little sophistication or perception can somehow smell manipulation. The conference leader who truly manipulates is doomed to fail eventually. In this illustration, the leader did not manipulate the participants, although he did lend his prestige to what he considered a rational and appropriate way of dealing with the issue. The conferees could have rejected this leadership if they found it inappropriate.

The conference leader has the opportunity to direct the conference by his choice of agenda as well as by his leadership during the conference. He does have a clearly defined responsibility to gather the most capable and appropriate resources to solve problems, and he must meet this challenge through the use of every leadership skill he possesses.

In the actual running of the conference, the leader must deal with a number of problems: (1) hostility toward him or other members; (2) rejection of his leadership; (3) strong, opinionated conferees determined to achieve their own goals; (4) illogical but highly articulate conferees; and (5) silent, potential noncontributors.

Hostility is difficult to deal with during the conference, but the leader must never reciprocate the hostility. Rather, he must deal with it patiently and courteously. Hostility between conferees can best be handled with comments like, "I am sure Bill didn't mean it that way," followed by an explanation of the point to soothe both sides.

The rejection of leadership requires the leader to obtain the support of other conferees, even if that means isolation of the rejecter and the buildup of his hostility. The conference leader must guard his position tenaciously, except when the usurpation proceeds in the right direction. At the appropriate point, he can easily reassert his leadership by using the summarization technique.

The strong, opinionated conferee usually has a hidden agenda of points he wants to achieve. The experienced conference leader can usually predict this type of action in advance and attempt to deal with it before the conference. He can try to develop the agenda with the help of this conferee to effect some compromise that will permit discussion of all relevant issues. He can even make a special assignment to this man to provide a researched or well-thought-through position statement. Such an assignment could be made to a subcommittee, so that a strong opposing point of view could be taken by one of its members to counteract the adversary's position outside the conference. If the hidden agenda erupts during the conference, the conference leader must use summarization and similar techniques to ward it off. Finally, he may have to assert his position strongly and rule the issue out of order.

The illogical participant who attempts to dominate the discussion is quickly rejected by the other conferees, but it is difficult for them to shut him up. One method that the conference leader can use is to call on people by name as an alternative to freer, more open discussion which is quickly dominated by the incessant talker. Another method is the head-on collision, in which the conference leader says, "There are a lot of people we haven't heard from," and then states that people should wait until others have been heard before venturing additional opinions and information. Finally, he can raise a point of order and ask that people be recognized from the chair before talking, and simply not call on the incessant talker.

The quiet, nonparticipating conferee can be handled by similar techniques—calling on conferees by name, going around the conference for individual remarks, and even by a statement such as, "We have heard from some of you quite a bit, but there are others who have had little chance to contribute," or "Let's ask those who have been talking to keep quiet for the next half-hour so we can hear from the others."

The effective conference leader will develop a number of these techniques over time. But he must still listen very carefully to everyone, sort out and analyze statements to relate positions of conferees to the solution of the problem, and avoid dominating the conference or inhibiting free and open discussion.

Step 6: Terminating the Conference. The termination of a conference is as critical as any of the other steps. The participants do not want a conference ended without some resolution of the issues and problems. On the other hand, there is a limit to their attention span. The conference leader must size up the situation and act forcefully to reach final accord and adjourn the conference. However, premature attempts for consensus or summary will be rejected by the group, and the leader may have to summarize and set forth the remaining unresolved issues. The critical point is that he must exercise leadership in stating what the conference has accomplished and what is yet to be achieved, and then move in an orderly fashion to termination.

The assignment of special tasks to individual members is an appropriate way to develop position or working papers for the next conference. The leader must be sure, however, that he has the power to make such assignments, and he usually should not make them before discussing them with the people concerned. In this way, the leader not only indicates his awareness of the participant's many other responsibilities, but also builds a cooperative spirit with the group. When individual assignments are made, they should be confirmed in writing after the meeting, and recorded in any minutes that are kept of the proceedings of the conference. Each assignment should include both a deadline and some specifications as to the scope of the problem to be investigated. The assignment can be given either to an individual or to a subcommittee of two or three members.

Step 7: Followup on the Conference. Individual conferees usually enter into a conference in good faith and give all their skill, attention, and expertise to it. The conference leader may have handled the conference expeditiously with the appropriate summaries and consensus, but afterward there is usually no formal mechanism to assure the conferees that action has been taken on the recommendations or solutions they proposed during the conference. Although managers are usually so busy that they rarely have time to find out whether appropriate followup was made, they nevertheless experience a nagging doubt about how much can ever be accomplished by committees or conferences. This doubt will condition the conferee to be less involved in succeeding conferences, and should be dispelled by followup actions taken by the conference leader.

If the committee or conference is not a standing or permanent part of the management process, a document should be prepared and sent to each member. It should indicate the acceptance or rejection of the actions recommended in the conference, including the reasons for any rejections. Some managers worry about opening a Pandora's box and feel that it is best not to let conferees know if their ideas have been rejected. But this attitude assumes that no other sources of information exist in an organization which will inform conferees of action or lack of action. If the committee is a permanent one, the minutes of the meeting and special periodic reports will suffice to keep the conferees apprised of actions taken as a result of the meetings.

Role Expectations and Conference Leadership

The actions of the conference leader are the most important attributes of conference dynamics. He must condition his behavior to meet the role expectations of the conferees rather than exercise his own personality and leadership style. The role expectations are usually sufficiently diverse to give the leader considerable latitude in developing his conference leadership style. But there are some basic factors involved in role expectations which are critical to shaping that style.

The conference leader cannot dominate the group with his own opinions (except the informational conference), or he will stifle any useful discussion. This domination can take many forms, even to the point of how often he speaks. In some ways, he is like the coach of an athletic team; he can provide direction from the sidelines but he cannot call the actual plays on the field or hold a major position on the team himself.

The conference leader cannot abandon leadership, since he will be blamed for failure to move in an orderly fashion to solutions and for failure to develop viable alternatives and solutions to the problems or issues. The group expects the conference leader to prohibit lengthy discussions of tangential issues, to provide the opportunity for all to be heard, and to prod the group gently toward discussions of substance of the issues at hand.

Conference leadership is a most difficult role which is rarely done well. To provide leadership without domination is to draw a very fine line. But the manager who recognizes the dimensions of the group dynamics involved in conference leadership can acquire considerable insight on how to draw this fine line, and will be a more effective conference leader.

9

Leaders are made, not born. To become a leader it is necessary to develop leadership skills, which are in turn founded on a deep and pervasive understanding of human beings and human behavior in organizations. To translate this knowledge into effective leadership requires insight, which can be gained only through constant analysis and reevaluation of everyday interpersonal relationships.

Developing Leadership Skills

THE LEADERSHIP ROLE in business organizations results from the appointment of managers rather than from a natural selection process through group action. Thus, the leader is beholden more to the organizational hierarchy than to his followers or subordinates. A set of role expectations apply to any leadership position, both from the leader's leader and from his followers. Primarily, these role expectations are an asset rather than a liability for the manager as leader, since they create a situation where prior experience has conditioned others to accept rather than reject leadership. Furthermore, the leadership role usually offers the leader opportunities to utilize existing reward and punishment systems to ensure his acceptance.

An extreme illustration of this conditioning process took place during World War II. A group of Allied soldiers, who were dressed in German uniforms and told to speak only in German or in heavily German-accented English, gained access to an Allied intelligence headquarters in England and left with classified information. When the Allied guards were asked why they admitted the obviously foreign soldiers, they replied that the men's leaders seemed to be officers, and that the guards assumed that the uniforms were Norwegian and that the men were undoubtedly Allied soldiers on a special mission. The role expectations of the Allied soldiers conditioned them to accept the leadership of officers, even when they did not know them and were not even able to identify the uniforms.

Although there is a potentially high degree of acceptance of the leadership role by subordinates, this is only one plus among many minuses. A new leader creates uncertainty, which is one of man's potentially greatest causes of anxiety. This uncertainty is not only task oriented but also personality oriented, since subordinates dread potential personality conflicts, the possibility of favoritism, and all the dimensions of social and behavioral changes. They adjusted to the previous leader, even though he might have been unsatisfactory. They developed methods to compensate for his lack of decisiveness, or his tendency to blame others for his own shortcomings. They may not have liked him or his methods, but they *understood* him, therefore greatly reducing uncertainty.

Let us consider the role-expectation problem of a new leader who has been appointed to an important position in a company. He has been hired from the outside, has a fine record of achievement, and seems to be a very fair man, although demanding of his subordinates. The first factor is that the grapevine has been busy searching out background material and is usually inclined to accept the negative rather than the positive features about this man. In this instance, the grapevine stresses the demanding aspect of the man's managerial behavior, embellishing it to make him an ogre who has dismissed people right and left. The company executives realize the potential disadvantages of the grapevine accounts and counter them with a release on the new manager, noting all his accomplishments. But the release cannot say the reassuring things, such as the fact that the man has a reputation for working well with subordinates, and that although he has dismissed some men, they were only a few and they deserved it. Such a statement would be likened to "There is no truth to the rumor that . . ."

The anxiety has started and rumors will build to a pitch before the new manager actually takes over the job. Some insecure employees might even act on the rumors by looking for new jobs. This would be an extreme situation, but it could occur. When the new manager takes over, he must move quickly to dispel any notions that he is going to effect wholesale dismissals or drastic changes without working with his subordinates.

One way for the new manager to offer this reassurance is to hold an initial group meeting to discuss his methods and how he plans to exercise leadership. This technique has the advantage of quick action, but the disadvantage of not really establishing communication. Yet it may be necessary if the grapevine has been particularly unkind to the new manager. A better way is to schedule interviews immediately with key subordinates on a task-oriented basis. The manager should indicate his interest in finding out what the problems are, what approaches have been used in the past, and what his subordinates think about key issues.

The role expectations to this point have centered around the creation of uncertainty by the appointment of a new manager. These expectations have been primarily negative. In general, however, role expectations about the leader tend to have positive elements as well. Subordinates accept the power of the authority vested in the leader by the managerial hierarchy. A new manager is known to have the potential for giving raises and making promotions, and also for taking punitive action for poor performance. This power dimension extends to the acceptance of the manager's ability to institute change through his relationship with the managerial hierarchy, and when the subordinate himself initiates the change, he is desirous of his leader having such power.

But the new leader must also guard against placing too much faith in the positive factors supporting acceptance of his leadership. One example of this occurred when an old-timer in a relatively important position had a discussion with his newly appointed leader. The latter painted a glowing picture of the excellent things he was going to do and how wonderful these changes would be for the old-timer. Then, noticing the employee's lack of enthusiasm, the manager asked, "Why aren't you pleased about the potential of these far-reaching plans for you and the company?" The old-timer replied, "In the past ten years, five people have sat in your seat and told me about the wonderful future, and I have reached the point in my life where I can wait until you actually have done all these things before I get enthusiastic."

A new leader can learn from this interchange that deeds, not talk, will convince subordinates to put their trust in his leadership. In the long run, the leader role expectations of subordinates, although rarely articulated, relate mainly to the relationship between the individual and the leader.

Decisiveness and Command. The subordinate expects the leader to be more proficient than he is, particularly in his managerial acts. Although the subordinate may have poor self-perception and therefore rate himself as superior, when he comes to the leader with a problem, he expects him not only to be able to solve it but also to initiate action toward its solution.

Acceptance of Responsibility. The subordinate wants a leader who faces up to his responsibilities and accepts them. He is fearful of the leader who shirks responsibility or who looks to others to accept the blame for mistakes. The leader who constantly blames his superiors for their failure to do what he thinks is right weaves a web of incredibility and weakens his relationship with his subordinates.

Fairness in Evaluation. Many people have a deep feeling that evaluation does not take into account their special problems and qualifications. Very early in life one realizes that evaluation is constantly being made on every action one takes, from an arithmetic test in the third grade to consideration for a merit pay raise on the first job. Because it is difficult to persuade others that an evaluation is being done fairly, performance appraisals in industry have come under heavy attack.[1] Since people automatically personalize evaluations, the leader should set up objective measures, primarily task oriented, against which to measure performance. In addition, he should allow ample opportunities for dialog and discussion, not only at the time of the formal appraisal but also during the normal course of the work week.

Rational and Consistent Approach. The emotionless leader is usually not well accepted, but the irrational, highly emotional leader is rejected. The concept of consistent behavior is important, even if that behavior is unsatisfactory, because it reduces uncertainty. Followers like their leader to feel emotion, but not to act emotionally. In other words, they want him to keep his cool.

[1] A typical example of the newer approach to evaluation appears in John B. Miner, "Bridging the Gulf in Organizational Performance," *Harvard Business Review* 46 (July–August 1968), pp. 102–110.

Competence. It is important that subordinates perceive the leader as competent in his field of expertise. This applies particularly to subject-matter fields; it can create inane situations, as when a research laboratory must be headed by a Ph.D., or a hospital staff by an M.D. The leader who does not have the competence expected by his followers will have great difficulty gaining acceptance.

Intelligence. The leader is expected to have a higher intelligence than his followers, but not too much higher. The leader whose intelligence greatly exceeds that of his followers will be rejected, partly because the difference in intelligence creates a communication gap, but mostly because it creates a feeling of inferiority, causing the followers to fear the leader's potential contempt for them.

Results Orientation. Groups vary in their demand for freedom of personal action and the desire for structure, but any group formed to achieve a task becomes highly frustrated when that goal is not accomplished. A classic example of this appeared in Feodor Dostoevsky's account of a Czarist Siberian prison camp in *House of the Dead*. When the prisoners were not assigned a task, morale was low, work performance slovenly, and the accident rate very high. This was true even though the only reward for task achievement was a work day of slightly fewer hours and return to a bestial prison. But when they received a task assignment, the men worked with a will and showed satisfaction from task accomplishment.

Openness and Accessibility. The term "openness" may connote a relationship which is not necessarily acceptable to either the leader or the followers. The climate of the firm may not lend itself to a degree of openness, and the traditions of management may reflect rigid and guarded interpersonal contacts. Openness in such a climate may become suspect and result in deterioration of the relationship between leader and follower. Perhaps a better term might be "trust" or "honesty." The follower wants to feel that the leader's word is inviolable and that he can depend on it, no matter what happens.

Accessibility is also an important means of developing trust. The term "open-door policy" could be applied, although sometimes it is used by the president or other higher executive to imply that he will see anyone at any time, a practice which can lead to a breakdown of the entire hierarchical system. Such an open-door policy creates a feeling of uncertainty in the manager whose subordinates choose to see the president, and if the president acts on information he receives from them, he will be violating his own managerial hierarchy. If he fails to act on the information, then nothing has been accomplished except greater frustration for both the lower followers and the lower leaders.

In contrast, the use of an open-door policy to promote the manager's accessibility to his own followers will not cause such danger, and will create a bond between them. However, if accessibility is to become a reality rather than a myth, the leader must be a good listener and be willing to spend the necessary time with his subordinates. In one case where a follower came in to see his leader, the latter told the man to sit down and talk, while he continued shuffling papers and signing letters. The follower became so exasperated that he jumped from his chair and said heatedly that he would come back some other time. The leader asked why, and when the subordinate indicated that the manager was obviously not listening, the latter recapitulated all the points raised by the follower. This did not satisfy the man, who said, "Hell, I don't care if you did hear everything I said. I felt you were not listening and therefore were not interested in talking to me."

The Leadership Role and Organizational Expectations

The leader not only has follower expectations but also organizational expectations. He is appointed to his job to achieve certain tasks or goals. The organization sets forth a number of requirements or expectations for the leader to satisfy, although the majority of these are implicit rather than explicit.

Conformity to the System. The leader can change the system over time but cannot be in conflict with it. The system demands conformity, even to the choice of language and dress. Fortunately, many of the irrelevant signs of conformity are being relaxed, mainly in the social areas such as make of car, sartorial and tonsorial styles (within limits still), and the conduct of one's private life. But task-oriented conformities have not been relaxed, and standards relating to hours of work and relationships with peers and superiors are still very rigid.

Achievement of Results. The more progressive business firms are moving toward greater and more precise measurements of results. The leader accepts budgets, cost limitations, and time constraints as part of the system, and he accepts the need for achieving results or tasks to which he has agreed regardless of those constraints. Excuses for nonperformance are simply not acceptable in today's business firm, even if the excuses are logical and sound. The leader is expected to bargain for the necessary resources to achieve the task, and once he accepts the task, he will be held to it.

3. *Loyalty to His Boss.* Disloyalty is one of the cardinal sins of business, and is rarely tolerated. This reduces the options open to the man who is dissatisfied with the leadership provided him. He can create a crisis situation by demanding the removal of his boss, which usually has little chance of success. He can wait until it is obvious to everyone that the boss is incompetent, but he himself may be swept out with the broom of the newly appointed boss. Or he can decide that the situation is intolerable and seek employment elsewhere.

4. *Nondrastic Action.* The results-oriented leader is often faced with inadequate or inappropriate resources to achieve the task. He can bargain for greater or new resources, but there is a limit to how far he can go in his demands. If the requested authorizations are drastically different from those of his predecessor, the leader faces the possibility of censure, although such measures are usually informal rather than formal. One of his greatest problems is the reallocation of the human resources assigned to him. It is difficult to get rid of unsatisfactory subordinates, especially if they have long tenure or if there are too many of them. If the leader replaces one or even two subordinates in a relatively short period of time, this action will be tolerated if he is also producing results. But when the number exceeds two or three, the leader himself is in grave danger of being censured or disciplined in some way, even though he might be achieving results.

The Leadership Role and Personality

It might be stated that the ideal leader is a programmed automaton, who has no personality factors which would destroy his effectiveness, and who always can and will take a rational and calculated approach to all problems. Certainly the leader can rarely afford to indulge his own personality when it detracts from his leadership role. But is this a realistic profile of a leader? Can he change his behavior patterns drastically? The answer is no. At most, he can change only his adaptive or outward behavior.

The manager, in developing his leadership role, should not attempt to adopt patterns that are foreign to his basic nature. For example, the Anglo-Saxon lives in a no-touch culture, and has difficulty adapting to the touch culture of the Middle East. If he had to develop a touch relationship, perhaps holding hands with a man in Arabian fashion, he would find it difficult and at most would utilize adaptive behavior patterns. He would probably be unable to adapt sufficiently to build deep relationships with the Middle Easterner. Similarly, the leader has certain ingrained behavior patterns, and he must examine every change very carefully so that he will not lose his effectiveness by adapting his behavior to an untenable way of handling himself.

One of the disadvantages of sensitivity training or T-groups is that the self-awareness the participant gains often creates a feeling of inadequacy, leading to the adoption of a totally alien behavior pattern. An aggressive and forceful man may realize through the training experience that these traits result in bruised feelings and even a feeling of dislike on the part of the other participants. He soul-searches to determine whether he can live with what the others consider to be unsatisfactory behavior, and may decide to make his behavior less abrasive. However, when he returns to his company, his subordinates face a new set of uncertainties. They had learned to live with the leader's personality characteristics, and they don't know how to deal with this stranger. The leader's superior is also at a loss because he had promoted this man on the basis of his aggressiveness and had compensated for his failings in the people he had assigned to the man and in the organizational structure he had designed.

This is not to deprecate the usefulness of sensitivity training or to tell every manager that he should not change his leadership role and patterns. However, the leader must exercise caution so that he does not adopt ways so alien to his own thinking that he loses his effectiveness. He should examine the role expectations of his followers and of the organization, and his own personality, to determine how he can adjust both to permit optimal effectiveness.

Organizational and Personal Goals

The leader faces a potential conflict of organizational and personal goals both for himself and for his subordinates. The organizational goals override the personal goals, since the organization is an impersonal entity with highly specific goals and built-in rewards or punishments for their achievement. Business exists to produce goods and services by utilizing resources allocated to it. Its reward for effective accomplishment is profit (defined as output exceeding input), and its punishment for failure to accomplish the task is bankruptcy. Each employee is but one of the input resources who may or may not achieve his personal goals from membership in the firm.

How is the leader to exercise his role of accepting the potential conflict between organizational and personal goals? In many ways, there is a great resemblance between the two sets of goals:

Organizational Goals	*Personal Goals*
Stability	Certainty of employment
Growth	Individual growth
Profit (really a means rather than a goal)	Economic viability
Survival	Human dignity

But there is a conflict of means as well as goals. The organization must rely on a high degree of compatibility among its parts, and therefore on consistency of behavior, while each man wants to assert his individuality and his personal creativity. This leads to a conflict, since the firm wants to organize people toward a common way of doing things. This dependency-independency issue lies at the heart of many conflicts between organization and the individual. McGregor advocated his Theory X–Theory Y dichotomy to dramatize management's failure to allow independent individual action by forcing dependence.[2] For years Argyris has believed that this conflict cannot be resolved, although he advocated a modification of the organizational structure for increased employee participation in a "mix model."[3]

[2] Douglas McGregor, *The Human Side of Enterprise* (New York: McGraw-Hill Book Company, 1960).

[3] Chris Argyris, *Integrating the Individual and the Organization* (New York: John Wiley & Sons, Inc., 1964).

The leader is both the master and the servant of the conflict between goals and means. He is master, since he has some control, even if limited, over the organizational structure, work assignments, and the opportunity for greater freedom of action. He is also servant, since he too is controlled by the overall design and intent of the organization.

In addition, the leader must relate his personal goals to those of the firm, and may have difficulty doing so. The organization has some immediate needs which often do not and cannot take the individual needs into account. A prime example of this situation occurs when an employee is retained in a job and his promotion deferred because it would be catastrophic for the organization to lose his services in that job in the short run. When the leader encounters this situation, either for himself or for one of his subordinates, he is expected to take a longer-run view of it and not be upset over the shorter-range action. But this is asking a great deal of a man, and often the explanations are far from complete. The solution to this problem is to provide greater balance between the organizational and the individual needs by giving the man the choice of whether he stays on the highly sensitive job for the short run or takes the promotion now. One could argue that this is no real choice, since the organization will long remember his selfishness if he chooses the promotion; still, the choice is made *by* the man concerned, and not *for* him.

The leader must build in more individual choice and freedom of action for his subordinates if he is to prevent their apathy and withdrawal. The freedom cannot be absolute, since organizational needs must also be stressed if task accomplishment is to be achieved. But there is much more flexibility in most organizations than most leaders are currently utilizing. One of the leader's main tasks is the resolution of conflict, not only between individuals but also between the individual and the organization.

Structure and Freedom of Action

Closely akin to the conflict between organizational and personal goals is the internal conflict within the individual between a desire for freedom of action and a desire for structure. This is depicted in

The Evaluation Process

In the final analysis, the leader can only be as effective as the people who work for him permit him to be. It is possible for him to replace some of his people, and even in extreme instances to replace all of them. He can wield power and coerce adaptive behavior from his followers. He can buy acceptance to his wishes through bribery or favoritism. But these are probably effective only as short-term tactics, since they are not based upon respect, loyalty, and real acceptance of the leader.

The road to those three desirable qualities is paved not with popularity or love, but with understanding, trust, and effective communication or dialog. A major stumbling block to these is the evaluation process. Evaluation connotes judgment as well as potential exposure of oneself to emotional probing by others. A typical appraisal interview illustrates this problem.

> LEADER: Bill, as you know, I have this appraisal form to complete on you. Here is a copy for you to look at while we go through the appraisal. But let me tell you right now, Bill, personally I think very highly of you. Let's go to the first item—loyalty. Now that is where you absolutely shine [the leader continues down the list, commenting on each item in turn]. Now, let's look at my suggestions for improvement. One of the things I feel is that you need to get along better with others. Frankly, this last year we had more friction than is right.
>
> FOLLOWER: I don't know what you mean about getting along with others. When have you had any problems with me? You know that Smitty has always had it in for me—you've said so yourself. I get along with most of the guys. Anyway, look at your own problems with Smitty.

What is happening in this appraisal interview? The leader has tried to discuss the subordinate's strong points first, but obviously is considering the form a matter of routine and giving little weight to the specific items. The subordinate recognizes this, and therefore pays little attention to the praise he has received on a number of the items. The leader then moves to the section covering suggestions for improvement and essentially attacks the follower on his inability to get along with others. The hostility evidenced by the follower indicates that he is quite surprised, and he then enumerates a number of situations where the leader has had his own problems. What is the result of this appraisal interview? Undoubtedly, it will be hostility, a lack of trust in the leader's judgment, and possibly even a breakdown of dialog or communication between the two men.

What was the cause of this failure? Part of it was the dependence of the leader on a formal appraisal or evaluation system in dealing with his subordinates. The leader needs to appraise and evaluate not on a periodic basis every six months or year, but daily and weekly. The purpose of the appraisal interview and of the entire evaluation system is *improved performance*. It is not and cannot be a disciplinary device in terms of punishment for nonperformance. Industrial discipline, and hopefully all discipline, can be justified only in terms of improved performance. Constructive discipline is an amalgam of a number of component parts which aim at modifying behavior, instilling a sense of responsibility, building consistent behavior, and so on.

Another factor that contributed to the failure of the appraisal interview were the tactics used by the leader in attacking the behavior patterns of the subordinate. It may have been true that the follower did not get along well with people, but he needed to be convinced of this failure before he could recognize its existence, and then he needed guidance on how to solve the problem. The manager must have known of specific incidents when the subordinate failed to get along with others, particularly if the leader had to step in to resolve the conflicts. That was the time for the leader to act to help the subordinate modify his behavior patterns. A man can deal far more easily with specific than with abstract situations, and especially highly emotional situations. The leader should not wait for a formal appraisal interview to solve problems that have been evident all year. Rather, he should move firmly and decisively to investigate the conflict, not only to solve it but also to prevent its recurrence.

Evaluation, then, is not solely a once-a-year formal interview culminating in a report to be submitted to personnel. It is the critical process through which the leader determines what action he must take to help the follower improve his performance. The evaluation involves not only those actions which have been performed unsatisfactorily but also those which have been performed well. Reinforcement of learning is one of the most powerful of all educational tools. The subordinate who is told that what he has done is right is likely to duplicate that action under similar circumstances.

The leader must guard against his own foibles in the evaluative probes. There is a tendency to a halo effect in judging total performance based on only one part of that performance. The leader could find that a subordinate is particularly persuasive and articulate, and judge all the other performance requirements on the basis of that ability. The subordinate may be lazy or sloppy in carrying through his tasks, but this weak point is so overwhelmed by his persuasiveness that the leader fails to recognize the weaknesses and take steps to rectify them. The halo effect can work equally on the negative side. Certain personality defects of the individual often color his relationships with his leader to the point where the leader is blinded to the man's good points. It may be possible to institute a long-range development plan to remedy the man's shortcomings. For example, some people are gruff and unpolished in their interpersonal relationships. This is usually the product of a long conditioning process in the man's family or in his educational and work experience, and the leader will need to take considerable time and patience to overcome these personality defects. But it is quite possible to isolate or insulate this man against work assignments when his personality defects would result in conflict and possible failure. In this way, the leader and the organization could capitalize on the man's strengths in the short run while attempting to remedy them in the long run.

A second foible of managers is to judge their subordinates on the basis of personality rather than results. Human beings are primarily emotional in their reactions to others, and tend to like or dislike people on solely emotional grounds. Over time this initial, highly emotional reaction is tempered by experience which dampens its extreme tendencies but does not eliminate them. The leader must be particularly careful in judging his followers on the basis of compatible personalities. He must work with a man he might instinctively dislike and produce the best possible results with him, regardless of potential personality clashes. One means to this end is to be much more oriented toward results and to determine whether the man is doing a good job. Another method is to discard the self-reference criterion which the leader uses to judge everyone else in relation to himself rather than in relation to his job. The yes man merely reinforces the personality and work characteristics of the leader, but does not complement them or compensate for them when they are inappropriate. It is much easier to live with a yes man, but the tenure of office will be considerably shorter and future promotion remote.

A third foible is to emphasize the present to the detriment of the future. Certainly one cannot be so future oriented that he neglects the present. But in developing followers through evaluation and appraisal, the leader must both plan for the future and deal with the present. Evaluation must be used as the major means for the development of subordinates. This requires a determination of each one's growth potential and the development of a plan of action to realize that potential. If the leader regards evaluation as a measure only of today's performance and is oriented toward characteristics required for improved performance only today, he is taking a short-run and dangerous approach to evaluation and development. What potential use does the leader and the organization have for the subordinate being evaluated? What characteristics does he have that eminently qualify him for his present job but are deterrents to promotion? For example, attention to detail is an admirable trait in a clerk but a potentially abominable characteristic for top management. The evaluation process must be broadened by the leader if it is not to act as a limiting factor on both his success and that of his followers.

The Counseling Process

The counseling process is inextricably tied in with evaluation but needs to be much more informal. In reality, the leader is primarily a counselor and a trainer, since his job is to organize others to achieve a goal. Certainly the organizational function involves many managerial and leadership skills, but the efficient handling of human resources will go a long way toward goal achievement. The counseling process recognizes the need for a constructive dialog between the leader and the follower with the objective of improved performance. It is the leader's role to institute counseling, not the follower's to seek it.

Counseling must start with an understanding of the subordinate that goes beyond the facade and probes more deeply into his motivations and human needs. The leader cannot be a psychoanalyst, but he can use some of the techniques of psychoanalysis to examine the emotional makeup of his follower. A caution is necessary at this point: Few leaders can be sufficiently skilled in the interpretation of psychological data and symptoms to provide true psychological help and advice. If the probing uncovers severe psychological problems, the leader must seek qualified help and immediately terminate his counseling role. The leader can seek to understand his follower better only to the point of looking at basic value systems and psychological needs that can be satisfied or are currently dissatisfied at work.

In today's more permissive world, many men probably have a higher aspiration level than is merited by their qualifications. When his aspiration level far exceeds his abilities, the average man becomes embittered and disillusioned. It is difficult for the leader to deal with a situation like this, but he must deal with it or face constant strife in his organization. One solution is to have frequent dialogs with the individual to help him see a broader picture of the world of work and his qualifications to compete. Another solution is to arrange a challenging opportunity for the subordinate in which he can prove to himself that he must either trim his aspirations or enhance his qualifications.

The leader as counselor must practice his listening skills to the highest possible degree. He can gain insight into his follower only by engaging him in dialog in which the brunt of the communication is carried by the follower. Once the leader has reached a deeper understanding of the individual, he can truly start a two-way communication to provide counseling and advice. The leader needs to use all his analytical powers to ascertain the real meanings or motives behind the points raised for discussion by the subordinate. A

Developing Leadership Skills

typical counseling session might develop considerable insight very quickly.

LEADER: Bill, I was just wondering about some of the things that have happened down on the production floor. You know, that business with Smitty.

FOLLOWER: Boss, if I told you once, I told you a thousand times, Smitty is just no good. All he ever does is make trouble for everybody else. Let me give you an example. You remember that situation with the parts shortage that Smitty blamed me for? Well, he didn't give me any warning that he was running out of parts. Yeah, I know he said that if I were just a little more civil, a lot more people would be willing to pass the time of day, and I would learn a lot. Anyhow, a system's a system, and it's up to everyone to make it work, and that goes for Smitty just like anyone else.

LEADER: Bill, does that apply to you too?

FOLLOWER: Sure, it applies to me. You know, come to think of it, maybe I am just as bad as Smitty in my own way. I want the paperwork to be perfect and when someone like Smitty fouls it up, I just get so damn mad that I forget about all of us working together.

This is an interesting illustration of the counseling process at work. Bill has little tolerance for anyone who does not follow the system down to the last piece of paper, and forgets that his function is to get the job done and not solely to service the paper system. By setting the appropriate stage, the leader has led Bill into discussing his own shortcomings rather than Smitty's. Undoubtedly the leader knew of Bill's intolerance but perhaps had not delved into its causes. He has learned that Bill believes that the system, and particularly paperwork system, is sacred, and that anyone who does not follow it is a traitor to the company. The leader could attempt to probe further into why Bill is so intolerant, but he must ask himself whether he has reached the point where he can counsel Bill sufficiently to overcome much of his intolerance. It is not the job of the leader to reform Bill and rid him of all his personal problems. It *is* his job to investigate those problems that cause ineffectiveness at work, except where such an investigation takes the leader into the discipline of psychoanalysis, from which he must retreat.

Counseling deals more with emotional than with rational problems. Facts might be involved, but usually it is the different perception of the same set of facts which creates the emotional problems. For example, the president of a company decided upon a special training program for one of his most promising young managers. The details of the program were worked out with him, and he was to spend a year at the opposite end of the country. On a holiday weekend a few weeks before the start of the training program, the young manager moved his wife and children to her father's home state, sold all their possessions, and started divorce proceedings. The president of the company regarded this action as evidence of a lack of maturity and judgment, and decided to cancel the training program. In the ensuing discussions, the young manager charged the company with a breach of faith, and stated that he and his wife had agreed to seek a divorce long before the decision about the training program. He further asked what possible effect his personal life could have on his business life. Eventually the problem was ironed out, but the emotional scars on both the young manager and his boss resulted in the former's resignation. The president's perceptions of the young manager's personal actions were themselves highly emotional, and the latter's perceptions showed a lack of experience and judgment, since he did not realize that his personal actions might be interpreted as a guide to his potential business actions. The emotional impact of both these perceptions might have been lessened had there been a counseling relationship between the president and his young manager. Undoubtedly this would have triggered a discussion of the latter's marital problems and their potential effect on his career.

Organizational Climate

Organizational climate is perhaps the greatest of all influences on leadership style and skill development. Leaders, especially when no highly organized leadership development program exists, learn about leadership skills by emulating their superiors. Collectively, this leadership style could be considered the organizational climate. Does the organization promote initiative or conformity? Is there a sense of openness or a widespread feeling of distrust? Is cross fertilization of ideas between departments encouraged or discouraged?

The organizational climate, or organizational character, as some have called it, is a reflection of the chief executive and his key managers, and of years of tradition and the development of a value system. The trained observer can almost sense the organizational climate from the decor of the reception office, and certainly from the first interview or contact with top managerial personnel. The major concern is to determine whether the climate inhibits or encourages individual improved performance.

Reward and Punishment System. Unfortunately for society, most organizations reward strict conformity to rules, regulations, and systems, and punish innovation. Budget behavior is one of the most widespread examples of this system. The budget is an excellent planning tool, but is used more often as a control weapon, with rewards for those who achieve budget and punishment for those who fail to do so. At the risk of oversimplification, there could easily be a situation where the individual has been punished by past failures to adhere to the budget and now refuses to take advantage of a market opportunity because it would involve exceeding his budget. Another example might be the contact individual who, in dealing with a customer, could take an innovative approach which would result in potentially high profits for the company but who has been conditioned by past punishment to adhere strictly to the letter of his instructions.

The point here is not that budgets or instructions are bad, but that there is a system which punishes people for any innovative actions. Certainly a company must protect itself against inappropriate actions by managers and employees, but an undue accent on punishment for mistakes will not necessarily prevent mistakes. Rather, it will condition employees to avoid any innovative action or interpretation of rules and regulations. This is particularly true in government, as noted in an article on the Bureau of Indian Affairs:

> The Bureau pays lavish attention to the wishes of the House and Senate Interior committees, and relatively little to the voices

of Indians that filter through the layers of BIA bureaucracy. And that is because there are few rewards for the bureaucrat who listens to Indians.[4]

Restrictive or Innovative Orientation. The organizational climate tends toward either an innovative or a restrictive orientation. Some companies establish elaborate and extensive company policy manuals, and an internal auditing system to ensure that managers and employees follow the manual. In one relatively large company, the policy manual called for all field operations expenditures over $250 to be approved by a series of steps culminating in approval at the vice-presidential level at the headquarters location. One field manager had a hole in the roof of his warehouse which would cost $750 to repair, and decided to follow this procedure. Although he marked the request urgent and sent it by telegram, the approval procedure was sufficiently cumbersome that he did not receive approval before his merchandise was damaged by the leaking roof. Russian industry is replete with thousands of similar examples, but how could this happen in a profit-oriented, private enterprise economy?

The explanation is quite simple, although it sounds absurd. The field manager had been conditioned to expect punishment for taking initiative and reward for following policy. Since he was not stupid, he knew he was taking a risk by not getting the roof fixed, but he considered that risk less dangerous than repairing the roof on his own initiative. During the subsequent inquiry, he was asked why he failed to make the repairs or at least to obtain immediate action from headquarters. He replied that he had sent a telegram but that he knew how important it was not to break company policy. The headquarters never intended company policy to be so restrictive that it would result in higher cost rather than in protection of the company against the poor judgment of field managers. However, the organizational climate had a restrictive orientation which resulted in the conditioning of managers to follow rules at all times.

It is difficult to develop an innovative orientation, particularly in large firms where there is great danger that innovation, if too widespread, could result in chaos. A managerial answer to this

[4] "Bureau of Indian Affairs: America's Colonial Service," *Look* 34 (June 2, 1970), p. 35.

problem has been decentralization, even in school districts like the mammoth Los Angeles City school system:

> A study prepared for the Legislature concludes that the district is seriously deficient in providing quality education, fails to afford adequate representation of residents, is lacking in cost efficiency, is not held accountable for performance, and has not achieved integration.
>
> The vast district is expected to be divided into smaller units as part of the most drastic decentralization plan in the country. The theory is that more localized control of schools is the answer to their ills.[5]

The critical issue is to develop an organizational climate which stresses an innovative orientation and rewards those who initiate new and better ways of doing things.

Participative or Authoritarian Management. The leadership styles of management are perhaps the most important ingredient in organizational climate. Although it is possible for a leader to utilize a leadership style quite different from those of other managers in the company, it is difficult to be totally successful with a different style. The subordinates will have been conditioned by the organizational climate toward one particular leadership style, and will find it confusing and even threatening if they have to adapt to a totally different style. Furthermore, the leader's boss will feel uncomfortable if his subordinate's leadership style is at variance with his own, and may even bring pressure to bear on the subordinate to conform to the more commonly accepted style.

Currently there is a tendency to equate participative with good and authoritarian with bad. It is really more appropriate to consider both styles as extremes and to find an acceptable middle position, *depending on the situation.* However, organizational climate is usually inclined toward one of those two positions, with considerable effect on the company. If the climate fails to encourage individual growth and motivation of subordinates through the appropriate leadership style, there will be an increase in apathy and

[5] "L. A. Schools May be Split into 24 Different Districts," *Los Angeles Times* 89 (June 7, 1970), p. 1.

withdrawal. Alternatively, if the climate stresses individual growth and motivation to the detriment of responsibility and a stress on results, frustration and perhaps even apathy will grow within the leadership ranks.

Universities have stressed a participative approach to develop a climate wherein faculty and students will feel free to make major contributions not only to their own disciplines but also to the organizational framework within which they work. This approach has produced a cumbersome and relatively ineffective committee form of organization, resulting in the stifling of concerted action toward organizational goals. This is not wrong, but the climate of universities stresses the participative role almost as an end in itself, whereas in the results-oriented business firm, the type of leadership style must be considered more directly in relationship to the firm's ability to achieve its goals.

Open or Guarded Interpersonal Relationships. Although individual employees may have great influence on whether relationships are open or guarded, the organizational climate will also affect how open people are with each other. If the organizational climate is receptive, openness can result in deeper trust and understanding among people, with resulting cohesiveness and cooperation toward common goals. If the climate is not receptive, the individual who practices openness may suffer personal difficulties and loss of position.

All the elements which constitute organizational climate are closely connected, and it is difficult to develop a participative management approach without greater openness in interpersonal relationships. For example, the climate of a firm which had sponsored a special management development course on interpersonal behavior had conditioned its management to accept an authoritarian approach and guarded interpersonal relationships. Thus, when the instructor tried to use pedagogical techniques to encourage both openness and participation, nothing happened. The result was that the instructor had to change his teaching techniques.

Goal-directed Orientation. An integral part of the organizational climate is its goal-directed orientation. Intense competition usually forces a firm to be strongly goal oriented to make a profit and maintain a market share. This goal-directed orientation becomes part of the organizational climate, which will then not tolerate nongoal-directed behavior. The climate may create aberrations where the goal-directed behavior is indirect rather than direct. An example would be the hours of work expected, or the expectation that a manager would travel on his own time on Sunday to an appointment on Monday, rather than taking a plane on Monday and arranging the appointment for Tuesday. The manager is more likely to be judged on his apparent behavior rather than on his results in reaching organizational goals.

Other firms, including natural monopolies such as utilities, have an organizational climate which tolerates nongoal-directed behavior to a much greater degree.

Cultural patterns also affect orientation. For example, in countries with a value system not based on the Protestant ethic, individual pleasure and goals will be accepted to a greater degree. This attitude may result in a long lunch hour and the sacredness of the uninterrupted long weekend.

In the great crisis over Hitler's reoccupation of the Rhineland in 1936, the British tradition of the nonworking weekend played a part:

> . . . the members of the British government had dispersed for the traditional English weekend. It was impossible to consult it. Eden made it clear to the French Ambassador in London that nothing could be decided in London until the following Monday, when the Prime Minister and his colleagues would be back.
>
> It was quite seriously believed in Berlin that Hitler timed his gambles in foreign policy for Saturdays, when he knew that the British cabinet ministers and other high officials were away from London observing their weekend in the country.[6]

The organizational climate plays an important part in determining which leadership skills managers will develop. In fact, it plays so important a part that the chief executive officer should be cognizant of the type of organizational climate in his firm and its effect on long-term growth and effectiveness.

---

[6] William L. Shirer, *The Collapse of the Third Republic* (New York: Simon and Schuster, 1969), p. 263.

The Development Process

The leader has two responsibilities for development: one to his subordinates and the other to himself. The former is a critical dimension in leadership, since the subordinate has no other formal means open to him to seek personal development. The leader holds the power to develop the subordinate within the organization, although the subordinate can seek to develop himself outside the organization through trade school and university study.

A number of factors affect the development of subordinates:

Self-motivation. There can be no development unless the individual wants to be developed. Development involves learning, which in turn requires input by the individual. The leader must not only determine whether his subordinate is motivated toward his own development, but must also use his persuasive powers to create motivation. The leader should be careful not to assume that all subordinates want development and eventual promotion, even though he himself may have those goals.

Intellectual and Other Abilities. Effective development requires not only motivation but also the ability to undergo training. This ability involves both intellectual capacity and what might be called aptitude or an appropriate set. Intellectual abilities differ greatly; some men are particularly adept at understanding and using abstract concepts, while others must deal with concrete matters.

Men also differ in their emotional appropriateness for a particular type of job. Some men can take stress, while others soon become neurotic and unhappy under the same conditions. Some are interested in meeting new people, whereas others dread new contacts. This emotional aptitude or set becomes one of the major constraining factors in the selection of individuals for development. The leader must know his subordinates well to ascertain their emotional appropriateness for particular types of jobs.

Opportunities for Development. The leader has only a certain amount of time available to devote to development, and a certain number of opportunities open to assist in the process. Training positions can be created—a lead hand on the production floor or a sales coordinator in the sales department—but they will necessarily be limited, and the leader must evaluate his priorities to determine which subordinates should be given the available opportunities.

Although he cannot deny development to the majority of his subordinates, development in total will be enhanced when he concentrates on those from whom he and the organization can receive the greatest possible return on investment. Of course he cannot neglect his other subordinates, but he will necessarily spend less time on their development.

The leader's second major responsibility is self-development. The highly motivated manager cannot depend on the organization to sponsor all of his development. Rather he must create his own development or career plan. This plan matches qualifications against opportunities to permit the manager to determine the optimal route to success in the organization. For example, in a typical food retailing company the primary route for promotion lies through the grocery department rather than through produce or meat. In a trucking company promotion usually comes through operations rather than through sales or finance. In today's rapidly changing business world, such observations might soon become obsolete, but it behooves the manager to determine his career plan on the best possible estimate of future conditions and future routes to promotion.

The manager must also determine what types of work experience are necessary for self-development and then persuade the organization to give him assignments which offer that experience. He can also upgrade his educational qualifications, either in a highly formal way through earning an M.B.A. degree, or through specialized courses with organizations like the American Management Association, or colleges or trade schools. These options are usually open to most managers without too much formal encouragement from the company.

Self-perception and the Self-audit

The leader must be highly critical of his own abilities to persuade and communicate with others, and to get a task accomplished. This requires self-perception—the ability to determine if the leader's view of himself and the world's view of him are the same. Man often deceives himself in order to live with his inadequacies and shortcomings, but self-deceit is dangerous for the leader because he may make decisions or projections based on false assumptions and perceptions. A number of factors contribute to false self-perceptions:

Hearing Only Yourself. There is a tendency for the leader to hear only himself instead of listening to others. He is used to commanding others and obtaining obedience. When he communicates, he hears himself very clearly as an articulate and knowledgeable man. He may even believe he is tolerant of dissension and willing to listen to others. In many instances, however, these self-images are not true. By listening to others, the leader will be able to perceive how they receive his communications and to build a more accurate image of himself which will enable him to deal with others far more realistically and successfully.

Overrationalization. All human beings must rationalize to live with themselves, but overrationalization can lead to a pathological inability to deal realistically with issues. In the leader, this overrationalization takes the form of writing off some of his subordinates, peers, and even superiors as unreasonable or unfair in their dealings with others. He does not take the time to investigate why he has these perceptions, but simply acts blindly on them in matters of conflict and failure. The leader must first look inward to determine if the fault lies within himself for his failure to deal effectively with others. Has he attempted to empathize with his adversary? What facts that he does not know could throw a different light on the problem? What personality traits are there in himself that may have alienated others?

Strengths Overshadowing Weaknesses. It is possible that the possession of a particularly important strength may blind the leader to some of his critical weaknesses. He may have a glib tongue and an unusual ability to impress others, particularly on first meetings, and yet not possess the necessary action orientation to carry through projects successfully. Since the leader in this instance feels that everyone likes and respects him, he may downgrade the importance of his failure to be action oriented, and eventually fail as a leader. No man is without faults, and it is difficult if not impossible to overcome every one of them. But the leader must be as aware as possible of his faults or weaknesses to determine if they are critical to his success. He may be able to choose subordinates who complement his weaknesses with appropriate strengths. The important point is that he be aware of his weaknesses and their potential effect on his performance.

Overdependence on the Momentum of Top Leadership. Some companies are characterized by good organization and leadership in the top echelons. These qualities make the jobs of lower leadership easier, because they can be carried along on the momentum of action and success which typifies the entire organization. The leader in the lower ranks may not be aware of how dependent he is upon this superior organization and management. For example, a company may have an elaborate management trainee program which produces well-qualified subleaders to support the lower leaders. Or the company may have a well-defined and operated management control system which provides timely and accurate information to permit lower leaders to take appropriate action to avoid errors. The leader in such an efficient organization may be lulled into a false sense of security about his own leadership abilities, which are really supported by excellent staff work and overall superior management.

The leader should realistically assess how much he contributes to the success of his part of the organization and how much is done for him. If he wishes to move into the higher echelons, he must be able to produce superior quality work under such support conditions. Through self-assessment he can determine what qualities he still must develop which would permit him to work in a less well-managed company, or to move up in his present company to a position where he originates the systems and methods of superior management.

The Highly Structured and Unreal World. The leader can build a wall around himself and live in an unreal world. He does not want to hear bad news, so he doesn't listen to it. He does not want to know that his subordinates are dissatisfied, so he doesn't talk to them enough to learn that. He can insulate himself by building an elaborate structure of authorities and responsibilities, even to the point of using his secretary to screen out potentially unpleasant interviews with his subordinates or peers. This leader is avoiding self-perception because he finds it unsettling and too emotional. But his wall will come tumbling down, and he will never understand what happened to him. No leader can afford to insulate himself, since it is far better to recognize a problem when it can still be solved than to wait until the solution passes into other hands.

The leader can give himself a self-perception test that will be extremely helpful to him in assessing himself. He should prepare a sheet with three columns. In the first column he is to list the traits on which he is to judge himself:

1. Openness
2. Tolerance
3. Arrogance
4. Loyalty
5. Interest in others
6. Self-confidence
7. Persuasiveness
8. Stubbornness
9. Ability to communicate
10. Leadership

He should give careful thought to what additional traits should be added. The second column should be headed "Your Perception of Yourself" and the third column should be headed "Others' Perception of You." The leader should complete the second column in some depth as realistically as he can. The third column should be completed over an extended period of time after listening closely and observing subordinates, peers, and superiors. The test should be considered confidential and shared with others only when there is assurance that such sharing will be helpful.

Another means of developing self-awareness is drawing up a personal balance sheet, in which the leader can list his strengths and weaknesses. Once the leader has completed his personal balance sheet, he should consider the importance of these strengths and weaknesses to his career plan. If the weaknesses that are revealed would prevent him from attaining his career plan, the leader should develop a two- to five-year plan of action for self-development to eliminate or at least compensate for these weaknesses. Both the self-perception test and the personal balance sheet need constant updating and honest reappraisal if the leader is to achieve continuing success.

Leadership skills can be developed, but their development requires great concentration and effort. The leader must translate his basic knowledge about human behavior and his abstract understanding of leadership into day-to-day leadership action for personal competence and task accomplishment.

Selected Bibliography

THIS BIBLIOGRAPHY in no way claims to be exhaustive, but is instead a short list of useful and important references which should prove interesting to readers of this book.

Patterns of Human Behavior

Berelson, Bernard, and Gary A. Steiner. *Human Behavior.* Shorter ed. New York: Harcourt, Brace & World, 1967.
Homan, George Caspar. *Social Behavior: Its Elementary Forms.* New York: Harcourt, Brace & World, 1961.
Kluckhohn, Clyde. *Culture and Behavior.* Edited by Richard Kluckhohn. New York: The Free Press, 1965.
Thompson, James D., and Donald R. Van Houten. *The Behavioral Sciences: An Interpretation.* Reading, Massachusetts: Addison-Wesley Publishing Company, 1970.
Zaleznik, Abraham, and David Moment. *The Dynamics of Interpersonal Behavior.* New York: John Wiley & Sons, Inc., 1964.

Motivational Theories

Herzberg, Frederick. *Work and the Nature of Man.* Cleveland, Ohio: World Publishing Company, 1966.

Likert, Rensis. *New Patterns of Management.* New York: McGraw-Hill Book Company, 1961.

McGregor, Douglas. *The Human Side of Enterprise.* New York: McGraw-Hill Book Company, 1960.

———. *The Professional Manager.* Edited by Caroline McGregor and Warren G. Bennis. New York: McGraw-Hill Book Company, 1967.

Zimbardo, Philip, and Ebbe B. Ebbesen. *Influencing Attitudes and Changing Behavior.* Reading, Massachusetts: Addison-Wesley Publishing Company, 1969.

Human Behavior in Organizations

Argyris, Chris. *Integrating the Individual and the Organization.* New York: John Wiley & Sons, Inc., 1964.

———. *Organization and Innovation.* Homewood, Illinois: Richard D. Irwin, 1965.

———. "T-Groups for Organizational Effectiveness." *Harvard Business Review* 42 (February–March 1964): 60–74.

Ginsberg, Eli. *The Development of Human Resources.* New York: McGraw-Hill Book Company, 1966.

Kelly, Joe. *Organizational Behavior.* Homewood, Illinois: Richard D. Irwin, 1969.

Lippitt, Gordon L. *Organizational Renewal: Achieving Viability in a Changing World.* New York: Appleton-Century-Crofts, 1969.

Sayles, Leonard R. *Managerial Behavior: Administration in Complex Organizations.* New York: McGraw-Hill Book Company, 1964.

Tannenbaum, Robert, ed. *Leadership and Organization: A Behavioral Science Approach.* New York: McGraw-Hill Book Company, 1961.

Weick, Karl E. *The Social Psychology of Organizing.* Reading, Massachusetts: Addison-Wesley Publishing Company, 1969.

Whyte, William Foote. *Men at Work.* Homewood, Illinois: Richard D. Irwin, 1961.

Communication and Conference Leadership

American Management Association. *Effective Communication on the Job: A Guide for Supervisors and Executives.* Rev. ed. New York: American Management Association, 1963.

Bellows, Roger. *Creative Leadership.* Englewood Cliffs, New Jersey: Prentice-Hall, 1959.

Selected Bibliography

Haney, William V. *Communication and Organizational Behavior: Text and Cases.* Homewood, Illinois: Richard D. Irwin, 1967.
Himstreet, William C., and Wayne M. Baty. *Business Communications.* 3d ed. Belmont, California: Wadsworth Publishing, 1969.
———. *Business English and Communication.* 2d ed. Englewood Cliffs, New Jersey: Prentice-Hall, 1970.
Maier, Norman R. F., and John J. Hayes. *Creative Management.* New York: John Wiley & Sons, Inc., 1962.
Sigband, Norman B. *Effective Report Writing.* New York: Harper & Row, Publishers, 1960.

Development of Leadership Skills

Bennis, Warren G. *Organization Development: Its Nature, Origins, and Prospects.* Reading, Massachusetts: Addison-Wesley Publishing Company, 1969.
Blake, Robert R., et al. *Managing Intergroup Conflict in Industry.* Houston, Texas: Gulf Publishing Company, 1964.
Brown, Ray E. *Judgment in Administration.* New York: McGraw-Hill Book Company, 1966.
Fiedler, Fred E. *A Theory of Leadership Effectiveness.* New York: McGraw-Hill Book Company, 1967.
Harrell, Thomas W. *Managers' Performance and Personality.* Cincinnati, Ohio: South-Western Publishing Company, 1961.
Jennings, Eugene E. *An Anatomy of Leadership: Princes, Heroes, and Supermen.* New York: Harper & Row, Publishers, 1960.
Likert, Rensis. *The Human Organization: Its Management and Value.* New York: McGraw-Hill Book Company, 1967.

Index

accessibility, need for, 160
accountability, lack of in delegation, 92
administrative assistant, power-hungry, 70
aggression, frustration and, 95
American management, changes in, 101–102
   see also United States
apathy
   communication and, 132
   decentralization and, 71–72
   human needs and, 10–11
Argyris, Chris, 7 n., 52 n., 164 n.
aspirations, vs. qualifications, 172
Atatürk, Kemal, 47–48
authoritarian leadership, 140
authoritarian management, vs. participative, 177–178
authority
   decentralization of, 18–19, 73–74
   defined, 26
   delegation of, 76–97
   in industrial environment, 26–30
   institutionalized, 27–29
   limits of, 7–8

   obedience to, 27–29
   power and, 26–30
   rejection of, 27
   usurping of, 92
autocratic leader, 59, 135
AVOs (Avoid Verbal Orders), 113

balance sheet, personal, 184
Barnard, Chester I., 25–26, 29, 33, 34 n., 52–53
barrier zone, in communication, 121
behavior
   counseling in, 95
   evaluation and, 96
   false premises in, 8–9
   leadership and, 1–21
   motivational patterns in, 42–43
   needs hierarchy and, 8–10
   perception and, 19
   simplistic explanations of, 11
   stereotypes of, 41
behavior change, frustration and, 99–100
behavior patterns
   control and, 111

behavior patterns (*continued*)
  in management policy, 98–111
  organization structure and, 63–74
Bell, Graham B., 5 n.
Bellows, Roger, 58 n.
Bennis, Warren C., 12 n., 104 n.
Berelson, Bernard, 34 n.
buck passing, organization and, 69–70
Burk, Warner W., 37 n.
business enterprise, status and, 32–34
business firms, social system and, 30
"businesslike" behavior, 7
business mores, evolution of, 7

Carey, Alex, 46 n.
castes, in India, 48
centralization
  computer in, 18
  vs. decentralization, 73–74
change
  criticism and, 49
  frustration and, 51
  resistance to, 47–51
Charlemagne, 54
Churchill, Sir Winston S., 56
civil service mind, 101
communication
  barriers to, 116–121
  changes in, 121
  from conference leader, 139
  control and, 111
  effective, 112
  good practices in, 133
  hierarchy and status in, 117–118
  interpretation of, 114
  leadership and, 112–133
  listening in, 125, 129–130
  in management by objectives, 111
  nonverbal, 128
  periodic audits in, 132
  persuasion through, 113
  playback in, 126
  prescription for, 128–132
  psychological aspects of, 130
  re-examination and re-evaluation in, 123
  rumor and grapevine in, 67–68, 132, 157–158
  social and institutional roles in, 118
  stereotyping in, 128
  symbolism and language factors in, 123–127
  two-way, 128
  well-being and, 119
  words in, 123–127
  written vs. oral, 113–114
  zones of, 121–123
communication behavior, understanding of, 127–128
communication filters, 115–116
company policy, conformity to, 101
company politics
  as influence, 39
  personality in, 36
complex organization, chain of command in, 67
composite theory, of leadership, 57
computer
  centralization and, 18
  decentralization and, 71
  human needs and, 73
conference
  follow-up of, 154
  group decision-making problems in, 142–143
  hidden agenda of, 152
  illogical or opinionated members of, 152–153
  informational, 140
  membership of, 136, 147–148, 152–153
  mixed-objective, 143–144
  planning of, 144–145, 148
  problem-solving, 141
  purposes of, 137
  running of, 148–153
  termination of, 153
  types of, 140–144

Index

conference leader
  climate created by, 138
  direction by, 151–152
  popularity of, 150–151
  types of, 135–136
conference leadership, 134–155
  membership and, 147–148
  problem definition in, 146–147
  role expectations and, 154–155
  style in, 146
conference leadership skills, developing of, 145–154
conflict
  in business situation, 8
  communication and, 118
conformity
  decision making and, 106
  social patterns and, 100–103
Constitution, U.S., 30–31
continuum, in manager-subordinate relations, 165–167
controls and control systems
  behavior patterns and, 98–111
  decision making and, 105–110
  evaluation in, 98
  frustration and, 99–100
  leadership and, 110–111
  motivation and, 103–108
  performance standards and, 110–111
  philosophy of, 108
  skills needed in, 110–111
  social revolution and, 105
counseling
  in delegation, 93–94
  leadership and, 171–174
Creative Leadership (Bellows), 58 n.
creativity
  desire for, 8
  leadership and, 53, 57
credibility gap, 117
criticism, change and, 49

Dark Ages, 54
decentralization
  behavior patterns and, 71–74
  controls in, 101
  goals of, 73–74
  problems of, 74
  self-determination and, 18
decision making
  conformity and, 106
  control system and, 105–110
  decentralization and, 72
  delegation and, 96–97
decision-making conference, 142–143
decisiveness
  of leader, 159
  in subordinate, 86
delegation
  vs. abdication, 86
  accountability and, 92
  authority usurpation in, 92
  care in use of, 84–86
  checkpoints in, 88
  controls in, 88
  counseling and, 93–96
  decision acceptance in, 96–97
  defined, 76
  direction in, 87, 90–91
  errors in, 85
  evaluation and review in, 88–89, 93–96
  factors in, 75
  failures in, 82–83
  faults in, 89–93
  four steps in, 87–89
  guideposts in, 87
  human needs and, 77
  indiscriminate, 81
  leadership and, 75–97
  leadership responsibilities in, 86–89
  leadership skills and, 84–86
  as leadership technique, 96
  management by objectives and, 111
  management skill and, 92–93
  organizational needs and, 78–79
  performance failure and, 82
  persecution complex and, 81

delegation (*continued*)
  planning and, 82–83, 88
  policy making and, 81
  rule of thumb in, 91–92
  skill in, 79–82
  vs. supervision, 84, 88–91
  supervisor and, 75–78
democracy, organizational entity and, 107–108
democratic equality, 15
democratic leadership, 58–60
Dichter, Ernest, 43 n.
Dickson, W. J., 46 n., 47 n.
direction, in delegation, 90–91

eager beaver, organization and, 69
Eden, Sir Anthony, 179
education, management philosophy and, 2
effective communication
  defined, 112
  prescription for, 128–132
  see also communication
effective organization, roadblocks to, 69–71
  see also organization
egocentricity, as communication barrier, 116–117
elite
  motivation and, 47
  status and, 33
emotional problems
  buildup of, 13
  counseling in, 174
empire-builder type, 69
entrepreneur, 102
environment
  equilibrium in, 48
  individual and, 43–45
equilibrium, vs. change, 48
esteem
  prestige and, 35
  status and, 30, 35
evaluation
  communication and, 117
  in delegation, 93–96

fairness in, 159
leadership and, 168–171
Evan, William M., 24 n.

father figure, as conference leader, 135
Fiedler, Fred E., 59 n.
Fiedler, S. E., 37 n.
Follett, Mary Parker, 28 n.
frustration
  aggression and, 95
  behavior change and, 99–100
  and resistance to change, 51

Gamson, Zelda F., 37 n.
Gandhi, Mohandes K., 48
Goldman, Ralph M., 24 n.
government, civil service concept in, 101–102
grapevine
  as communication, 132
  encouragement of by management, 67–68
Great Depression, 12
great man theory, 56
Gresham's law, 36
group
  formation of, 24
  heterogeneous, 24, 57
  homogeneous, 57
  relationships with, 5, 12–13, 52
  self-determination and, 17
  size of, 24–25
  as small-scale society, 61
group decision-making conference, 142–143
group members, task accomplishment and, 57–58
group mores, motivation and, 42
group needs, 12–13

Hall, Harry E., Jr., 5 n.
Hammarskjöld, Dag, 55
Harvard University, 46
Hawthorne experiments, 46–47
Hemphill, John K., 23 n.

Index

Herzberg, Frederick, 10 n.
hierarchy
  communication and, 117
  leader and, 156
  managerial, 7, 32
Hitler, Adolf, 179
Homans, G. C., 35 n.
homeostasis, 42
homogeneous group, 57
human behavior, *see* behavior
human needs, 8–14
  see also needs
human relations
  behavior knowledge and, 19
  in conference leader, 135
  lip service to, 3
Human Side of Enterprise, The
  (McGregor), 103–104

incentives, leadership patterns and, 41–62
  see also motivation
Indek, Bernard P., 24 n.
individual
  aspirations of, 53
  environment and, 43–45
  and informal organization, 66
  supreme goal of, 53
industrial environment, authority and power in, 26–30
influence
  company politics as, 39
  defined, 30
informal organization, 64–66
  dangers of, 66
  decision making in, 72
  as *fait accompli*, 68
  individual in, 66–67
  manager and, 65–68
  utilizing of, 64–65
  worker and, 68–69, 73
innovative orientation, 176
institutional role, communication and, 118
intellectual ability, 180
internal needs, 10

interoffice memoranda, 114
interpersonal relations, character of, 178
inventory control, delegation of, 90–91

Johnson Administration, credibility gap in, 117
Jung, Carl, 53

Kaczka, Eugene, 23 n.
Kelly, Harold H., 24 n.
Kelly, Joe, 6 n.
Kirk, Roy V., 23 n.

labor, as commodity, 1
language, communication and, 123–127
Lawrence, Paul R., 48 n.
leader
  autocratic, 59, 140–141
  competence in, 160
  consistency in, 159–160
  decisiveness and command in, 159
  equated with "manager," 2
  fair evaluation by, 159
  follower's needs and, 5
  intelligence in, 160
  loyalty in, 162
  nondrastic action by, 162
  openness and accessibility in, 160
  organizational hierarchy and, 156
  prime responsibility of, 57
  qualities required in, 159–161
  rational, 159
  responsibility of, 159
  results-oriented, 160, 162
  self-criticism by, 181–182
  self-perception and self-audit by, 181–184
  self-perception test for, 184
  unreal world of, 183
  see also manager
leadership
  attributes of, 34–39
  autocratic, 58–59

leadership (*continued*)
  behavior patterns and, 19–21
  communication and, 112–133
  composite theory of, 57
  conference, 134–155
  continuum in, 58
  counseling and, 171–174
  delegation and, 75–97
  democratic or participative, 58–60
  difficulty of, 3
  esteem or prestige through, 36–38
  evaluation in, 168–171
  freedom of action in, 165–167
  great man theory of, 56–57
  human behavior and, 1–21
  improved performance and, 169
  laissez-faire, 58–59
  manager and, 61–62
  need for, 2–3
  operational, 37
  opportunities for development in, 180–181
  overdependence on, 183
  participative, 58–60
  patterns of, 57–61
  perception in, 5–7
  personality factors in, 170–171
  persuasion in, 113
  role conflict and, 19–20
  role expectations and, 156–157
  schools of, 54–57
  situational, 55–56
  technological change and, 2
  theories of, 54–57
  traitist theory of, 54–55
  traits correlated with, 37
leadership pattern
  control and, 111
  motivation and, 41–62
leadership responsibilities, in delegation, 86–89
leadership role
  organizational expectations and, 161–162
  personality and, 162–163
leadership skills
  in delegation, 84–86
  developing of, 156–184
  list of, 110–111
  social system and, 22–40
leadership style
  delegation and, 79–80
  situation and, 62
Leavitt, Harold J., 25 n.
Likert, Rensis, 52 n.
listening, in communication, 125, 129–130
loyalty, 162

machine, man as, 1
man
  as machine, 1
  supreme goal of, 53
management
  early philosophy of, 1
  human relations lip service from, 3
  leadership failure of, 2
  manipulation by, 3
  recognition by, 15–16
  separation of ownership from, 102
management action
  human needs and, 10–14
  social system and, 39–40
management by objectives, 111
management controls, behavior patterns and, 98–111
  see also controls and control systems
management information, 67–68
management theory, authority in, 26
management view, integration with sociological, 25–26
manager
  action-oriented, 43
  authority limits and, 7–8
  communication perceptions and, 127–128
  control system and, 105
  counseling of subordinates by, 94–95
  creativity in, 8
  environment and, 61
  equated with "leader," 2, 61–62

Index

evaluation and counseling by, 94–96
institutionalized authority and, 29
limitations of, 6
listening ability of, 129–130
as "psychologist," 4
motivation in, 43–44, 51–54
needs identification by, 9
"relating" to, 3
and resistance to change, 50
results-oriented, 160–162
role conflict and, 19–20
role perception by, 77
social perceptions of, 5–6
subordinate interaction with, 165–167
supervision by, 76
task-oriented, 57
understanding of human behavior by, 19–21
see also leader; management; supervision
managerial hierarchy
authority and, 7
status and, 32
manager-subordinate continuum, 165–167
manipulation, by management, 3
manipulator, as conference leader, 135
Mayo, Elton, 46
McGregor, Caroline, 104 n.
McGregor, Douglas, 103–104, 164
Merton, R. K., 33 n.
Metcalf, H. C., 28 n.
Miner, John B., 159 n.
mixed-objective conference, 143–144
money, as motivation, 1
Moore, Leo B., 49 n.
motivation
as changing interaction, 53
control and, 103–108, 111
Hawthorne experiments in, 46–47
individual and, 43–45
leadership and, 41–62
manager's role in, 51–54
manipulation in, 3

money as, 1
needs and, 10–11, 53–54
patterns in, 42–43
sense of belonging as, 47
social approval as, 42–43
social status and, 15–16 (see also status)
of subordinate, 8
Munch, P. A., 33 n.

Nagel, Jack H., 27 n.
needs
delegation and, 77–78
determination of, 12
differences in, 12
group dynamics and, 54
group vs. individual, 12–13
identification of, 9, 13
management action and, 10–14
obstacles to recognition of, 13
recognition as, 14
nuclear age, personality in, 12

obedience, authority and, 27–29
open-door policy, in leader, 160–161
operations research, delegation in, 80
organization
administrative assistant in, 70
effective, 69–71
interpersonal relations in, 178
orientation in, 176–177
psycho-sociological factors affecting, 23–25
roadblocks to, 69–71
two views of, 22
organizational climate, 75, 174–179
organizational entity, participation and, 107–108
organizational expectations, leadership role and, 161–162
organizational goals, vs. personal goals, 164–165
organizational life, reality of, 28
organizational needs, delegation and, 78–79
organizational structure
behavioral patterns and, 63–74

organizational structure (continued)
  computer and, 71–72
  decentralization and, 18–19, 71–74
  esteem in, 35–36
  formal and informal, 64–65
  power-hungry types in, 69–71
  sociological view of, 22–23
  subgroups and, 25
  task-orientation view of, 23
organization man, conformity in, 100
orientation
  goal-directed, 178–179
  restrictive or innovative, 176–177
ownership, separation of management from, 102

Packard, Vance, 30 n.
Parker, Treadway C., 5 n.
participation, organizational entity and, 107–108
participative leadership, 58–60
participative management, vs. authoritarianism, 177–178
perception
  control and, 111
  leadership and, 5–7
performance
  control and, 110–111
  delegation and, 82
  improvement in, 169
permissive leader, as conference leader, 135
Perrow, Charles, 30 n.
persecution complex, 81
personal goals, vs. organizational, 164
personal growth, 10
personality
  as basis for evaluation, 170–171
  in company politics, 36
  leadership and, 163
personality growth, factors in, 12
persuasion, through communication, 113
physiological needs, 9
planning, delegation and, 82–83

Polansky, R. Lippitt, 37 n.
popularity
  in company politics, 36
  definition of, 37
  esteem and, 36–37
  influence and, 37
popularity seeker, as conference leader, 135
Porter, Elias H., 23 n.
power, in industrial environment, 26–30
power base, social system and, 31–32
power-hungry administrative assistant, 70
President (U.S.), authority of, 30–31
Presthus, Robert V., 28 n.
prestige, vs. status, 30, 33, 35, 38
problem-solving conference, 141–142
problem-solving group, size of, 24
promotions, personality and, 36
psychological threat, communication and, 119–121
psycho-social factors, in organizational structure, 23–25

racial integration, U.S., 48
recognition, need for, 14–16, 17
Redl, S., 37 n.
resistance to change, 47–51
responsibility, acceptance of, 159
restrictive orientation, 176
results, as leadership criteria, 160–162
rewards and punishment system, 175–176
risk, 102
Roethlisberger, F. J., 46 n., 47 n.
Rohrer, J. H., 37 n.
role conflict, 19
role expectations, conference leadership and, 154–155, 157
role perception, by manager, 77
Rose, Arnold M., 38 n.
rumor, as communication, 132, 157–158

Index

safety needs, 9
salesman, in informal organization, 66–67
scientific management, 1
security, change and, 60
self-audit, by leader, 181–184
self-awareness, balance sheet for, 184
self-determination, opportunity for, 17–19
self-fulfillment, 10, 17
  delegation and, 77
  as supreme goal of man, 53
self-motivation, 180
self-perception, 181–184
self-satisfaction, 57
sensitivity training, 6–7, 163
Sherif, M., 37 n.
Shirer, William L., 179 n.
situational theory, 55–56
small groups, characteristics of, 23–24
social approval, as motivation, 42–43
social needs, 9
social patterns, conformity and, 100–103
social perception
  need for, 5–6
  practicing of, 8
social recognition, 15
social revolution, control and, 105
social role, communication and, 118
social status, 15
  see also status
social system
  acknowledging of, 39
  delegation and, 83
  institutions and, 63
  leadership attitudes and, 34–39
  leadership skills and, 22–40
  management action and, 39–40
  model of, 31
  power and authority in, 30–32
society
  institutions of, 63
  status and, 32

sociologist
  management view and, 25–26
  small-group studies by, 23–24
soldier, disobedience in, 27
staff-line management, in organizational structure, 71
status
  in business enterprise, 32–34
  as byproduct, 38
  communication and, 117
  dangers of, 33
  elite and, 33
  vs. esteem or prestige, 30, 35, 38
  managerial hierarchy and, 32
  need for, 15
  vs. popularity, 36
  usefulness of, 32–34
status symbols, 34
Steiner, Gary A., 34 n.
stereotypes
  behavior and, 41
  in communication, 128
Stogdill, R. M., 37 n.
strength-weakness audit, 182–183
subcontracting, 65
subgroups, organizational structure and, 25–26
subordinate
  authoritative relationship with, 7–8
  counseling of, 94–95, 172
  decisiveness in, 86
  delegation and, 76
  development factors for, 180–181
  leadership needs of, 61
  leadership opportunities for, 180–181
  motivation of, 8
subordinate-manager continuum, 165–167
supervision
  vs. delegation, 84–85, 89–91
  excessive, 89–90
  manager's role in, 76
symbolism, communication and, 123–127

Kirtley Library
Columbia College
Columbia, Missouri 65216